MW00396421

KURT COBAIN

THE FALLEN ANGEL OF ROCK 'N' ROLL

whitestar

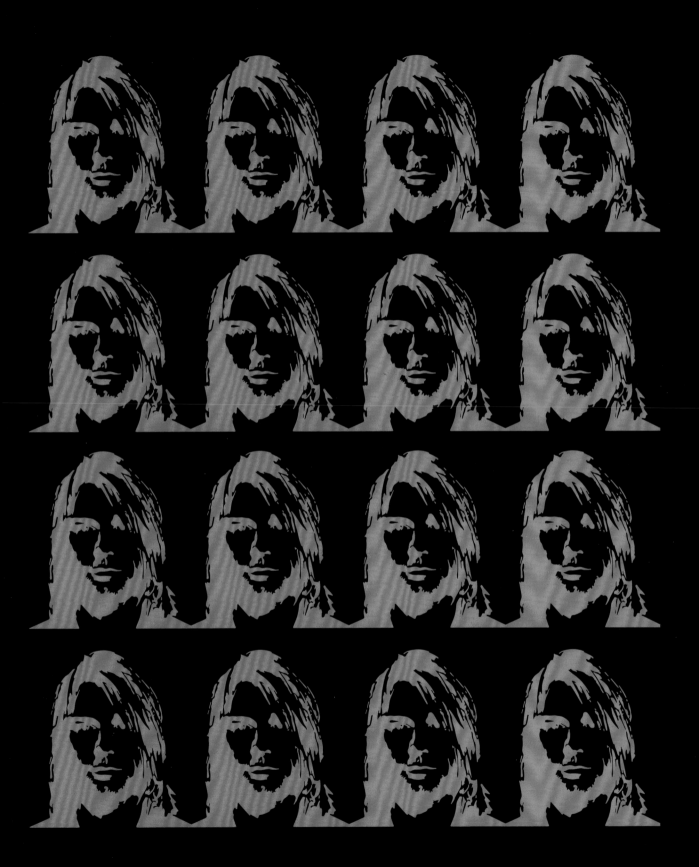

CONTENTS

It was the last big rock explosion. Of course, at the end of the day, rock 'n' roll didn't die after grunge: it's still alive and kicking in many ways. But the scene that cropped up in and around Seattle was without a doubt the last collective wave, the last global assault, the kind that could unite an entire generation around a certain sound, or better yet, an attitude, a mindset. Millions of hearts and minds spread around the world who, in that specific kind of music, saw themselves, felt reflected, felt some sort of kinship with one another, and, as a consequence, felt different from everyone else. Since grunge, only rap has managed to unite people in a similar way. Rock splintered off into countless streams, tribes, subgenres, and scenes, many of them ingenious, innovative and interesting, but

GRUNGE AND SEATTLE,
A PAIR THAT CHANGED
THE COURSE OF ROCK HISTORY

not quite able to speak to an entire generation. Not like grunge at least, the last of its kind. Is grunge a genre? No, although common elements identifying the "sound" of grunge are certain: the scope of punk, the power of hard rock and metal, the desire to combine it all with melody and lyrics.

Previous page: A close-up of Kurt Cobain, 1998.

Opposite: Kurt Cobain playing at the Reading Festival in England on August 23, 1992.

VANDALISM
BEAUTIFUL AS A B
IN A COR

There's nothing "English" about the attitude of grunge bands; their sound is undeniably American, deep in its roots. But the malaise that grunge expresses and places center stage, its rage, love, passion and desires, are shared by all of Generation X, tired of the hedonism of the 1980s and the legends surrounding the Baby Boomers, shared by a generation seeking introspection and perdition at the same time. A generation fighting against being condemned to invisibility.

It goes without saying that the two cornerstones of grunge are Nirvana and Pearl Jam. And, even if the Seattle sound extends far beyond just two bands, it's equally clear that the story and drama of the life of Kurt Cobain are central elements in the storytelling surrounding the phenomenon. Because of the songs he wrote and sang with Nirvana and the way he died, Cobain was—and still is—the symbol of the entire scene, the first rebel from the new white America, the last of the punks, the fragile poet of a generation and a young man constantly at risk. A symbol who, beyond his tale of love and success, beyond the happiness that he could have found in

THE LAST REBEL OF AMERICAN PUNK, THE FRAGILE ROCK POET OF AN ENTIRE GENERATION

his career and life, was always poised on the razor's edge, with one finger at the ready on the self-destruct button, as if in a spaceship in some science-fiction movie, a rocket launched into the rock heavens, with dreams, visions and galactic suffering and despair. The same suffering and despair that were with him up to his terrible end. On the other side of the spectrum, Eddie Vedder and Pearl Jam, the ones who channeled rage into art, poetry in rock, dreams into collective, passionate hope, into important political battles, into music not made for consumption. The ones who are still, stubbornly, here.

But here we'll tell the tale of Kurt Donald Cobain, born on February 20, 1967, a Pisces, in Aberdeen, Washington, USA.

Opposite: Nirvana backstage at Nakano Sunplaza in Tokyo, December 19, 1992.
Following pages: Close-up of Kurt Cobain's eyes in a photograph by Michael Lavine.
Pages 12-13: A promotional image from the With the Lights Out *box set, released in 2004.*

NIR

1

1967–1983
FAMILY, ADOLESCENCE & ABANDONMENT

THE ARTIST AS A CHILD
AMONG THE RUBBLE
OF A ONCE-HAPPY FAMILY

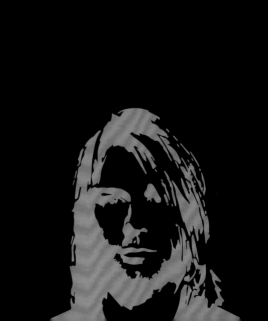

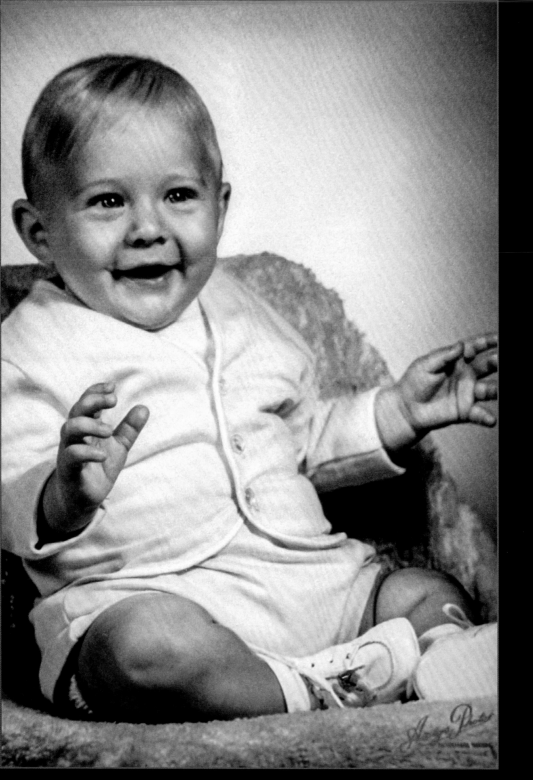

A normal adolescence? Not quite. Today it might be, but it wasn't in the early 1970s, when the world, when life in sprawling suburban America, was still conformist enough to be hard on a boy like Kurt. Like we said, he was born on February 20, 1967, at Grays Harbor Hospital in Aberdeen, a town in the state of Washington, the first of two siblings. His mother was Wendy Elizabeth Fradenburg (1948), waitress and secretary, and

Seattle remained unchanged in the sixties, far from the youth counterculture movement of the time

his father was Donald Leland Cobain (1946), a mechanic of Irish ancestry. They met at school and were married in Idaho in 1965, two years before Kurt was born. The first house that they rented was in Hoquiam, Washington; then, in August 1967, they moved back to Aberdeen, to 1210 East First Street, where Kurt's younger sister, Kimberly, came into the world on April 24, 1970.

Seattle had remained relatively untouched by the youth culture of the era, despite its proximity to vibrant California. There were a few hippy communes in Fremont and around the University of Washington, and young people certainly had fun at clubs and parties, but the music scene wasn't as thriving as that of the Golden State.

In any case, in 1967, something began to set in, and one month after Kurt was born, Seattle celebrated the Summer of Love with one of the Trips Festivals organized by Sid Clark, making way for hippies in the State of Washington, which, as we mentioned, didn't have much rock 'n' roll roaming its streets. The only local band that made it onto the lineup was Crome Syrcus, which was making a name for itself in San Francisco too. Then there were Don and the Goodtimes, founded in Portland by Don Gallucci, the ex-keyboardist of the Kingsmen; Emergency Exit from San Diego; and the stars of the era, the Electric Prunes, Jefferson Airplane and the Byrds, but not Jimi Hendrix, who in the meantime had moved from his hometown of Seattle to the more promising England. So, Seattle wasn't exactly a capital of rock and counterculture, and Kurt's parents were rather ordinary, especially when compared to their peers. The paternal branch of the family, originally from Ireland, wasn't particularly musically inclined, while the maternal side had a deeper relationship with the world of seven notes. And indeed, Kurt's maternal aunt Mari Earle Fradenburg was fundamental in shaping his destiny. A musician in her own right, she played guitar in a group that had gigs all over the county of Grays Harbor. She was the one who introduced him to music, ever since he was a young boy, inviting him to her band practice, having him listen to countless albums and, eventually, buying him his first guitar. Years later, she would even let him use her house as a rehearsal space and studio for his first raw recordings. Practically a manager, but on the lowdown. Even his maternal uncle, Chuck Fradenburg, played in a band called the Beachcombers, while his great uncle Delbert had a career as a tenor, even making an appearance in the

Page 16: The artist at one and a half years old.

Above: An image of the entire Cobain family: Kurt; his mother, Wendy; his father, Donald; and his sister, Kimberly.

At right: A photograph of Cobain at six years old.

1930 film *King of Jazz*, the musical that introduced jazz music to the white American masses, albeit in a "watered-down" form.

As we were saying, a normal adolescence up to a certain point. Kurt was a hyperactive, lively boy who struggled to concentrate. So much so that in 1974 his parents took his doctors' advice and started giving him Ritalin, a central nervous system stimulant that at the time was prescribed more often than it is today (thankfully so). But the family was doing well, Kurt was amiable, and everyone, aunts, uncles and grandparents included, loved him. However, the relationship between Kurt's parents began to be a bit less rosy in the early 1970s, and by the mid-1970s it began to deteriorate rapidly. They separated in 1976, when little Kurt was eight or nine years old. There wasn't a specific reason for the split; the two simply didn't get along anymore. As Kurt's mother later recounted, Donald practically wasn't ever home. Kurt's father left in March 1976; this abandonment, followed by his parents' divorce, was an event that was destined to have a profound impact on the life of the future singer. Kurt's mother in fact noted that, after their separation, her little boy's personality changed drastically; Kurt became an introvert and inclined to relate to the adult world through the screen of a provocative attitude. He would shut himself into long

silences, then he'd suddenly explode, often pounding on a drum that his father had left for him not long before the separation. And, seeing as bad and good always seem to incestuously intertwine in the lives of humans, perhaps we have this trauma to "thank" for Kurt the artist, as well as his humble and shy personality. "I was ashamed of my parents. I couldn't face some of my friends at school anymore, because I desperately wanted to have the classic, you know, typical family. Mother, father. I wanted that security, so I resented my parents for quite a few years because of that."

Kurt's mother, Wendy, could no longer keep up with her son's mood swings, in part because just a few months after the split with her ex-husband, she started dating Frank Franich, a man who proved to be violent towards her, a man whose behavior certainly didn't help Wendy's tendency to overdo it with alcohol. At times, Kurt had to bear witness to the violence inflicted upon his mother, which culminated in an episode in which Wendy had to be taken to the hospital for a broken arm. She refused to file charges against Franich and continued along in their relationship. Kurt went to live with his father. At first, things weren't so bad, in part because Donald felt a deep sense of guilt. He tried to form a good relationship with his son; he even promised him he'd never remarry. But the two didn't quite get along, especially because Kurt's father had moved to Montesano for work, and Kurt didn't exactly like the new living arrangements.

Kurt became moody and quiet, but he also began playing in the school band.

He enrolled in the Beacon School in Montesano, where he started playing sports (wrestling and baseball) and began attending band practice at school, playing the drums (and, to win favor with Kurt, his father even gave him a small drum set). But young Kurt was still moody and quiet, and he had trouble making friends. Donald tried to get him involved in different activities, taking him to work and even out hunting, listening to rock music in the car with him, but things didn't get much better. Actually, they got worse because Donald Cobain didn't keep his promise to his son: he started dating another woman, Jenny Westeby, and eventually had a child with her, named Chad. The two were married in June 1979. Donald, Jenny, Chad and Jenny's two children, Mindy and James, moved in together, essentially forming a new family unit.

At first, Kurt and his stepmother seemed to get along well, as she gave him the motherly attention he desired, but nothing was ever as Kurt really wanted it to be. His new life wasn't his old one, nothing ever returned to the right place.

Young Kurt Cobain plays the snare drum at an event at Montesano High School.

This new situation changed everything. Up until that point, despite the sudden mood swings and the isolation, Kurt had always been a shy, yet kind boy. But his character soon began to change, as he failed to find any other way to ease his pain and his sorrow over his parents' separation, no longer finding a familiar place that he could identify with, having also lost the exclusive attention that he enjoyed when he was an only child, or at least as the oldest son in the Cobain family. He grew increasingly insolent in relation to adults, and he began having tense relationships with some of his schoolmates too. Nothing too serious, of course, but just enough to convince his father and Jenny that he needed therapy. The therapist predictably told his parents that the boy essentially needed not to be bounced around from one family to another, that it would be good for him to live in one family environment. Both sides of the family then attempted to reunite his parents, without success. Failing to heed the advice of the therapist, the comings and goings between one house and the next continued, and Kurt even lived, for two short periods, with his aunts and uncles and, in particular, with his paternal grandparents, whom he had a great relationship with. "I truly was a loner. I wasn't interested in having relationships with other people," Cobain recounted. "I had a happy childhood until my parents got divorced, then all at once my world crumbled to pieces. I became antisocial, because I began to clearly see the environment I lived in, Aberdeen, Montesano, they didn't have anything to offer, no one was interested in what I was interested in, there wasn't anyone similar to me. I liked drawing, I liked reading, I liked artsy things and I liked music."

Kurt was a solitary teenager who just wanted to keep to himself

Leland Cobain, Kurt's grandfather, described him as a normal boy, who one minute was bored to death and in the next was hyperactive over a new artistic discovery. And he also liked music: "We had an old Hawaiian guitar and a small amp, and he had fun playing it."

As reported just about everywhere, the legend goes that at six years old, Kurt showed his drawings to his grandfather Leland, boasting that he could draw Mickey Mouse perfectly, even without copying from an already completed image. Leland, having seen the drawings, decided that they had to have been traced from the pages of a comic book, so Kurt redrew a perfect Donald Duck and Goofy, from memory, right in front of him, proving himself. Naturally, Leland was stunned by his grandson's gift. Grandpa Leland always then wore a watch with a dial featuring a small Mickey Mouse. In this talent, Kurt found unexpected support at school from his teachers, who appreciated his artistic capabilities, even if they objected to some of his drawings, which were often ironic and caustic, perhaps too much so for a boy his age. Kurt got out all the anxiety he had over his parents' failed marriage through sketches and comic strips. And in class all he did was draw: one of his schoolmates, Nikki Clark, once noted that the "future punk" Cobain really liked to portray subjects that tended towards the forbidden, with violent scenes, monsters and demons. They were the kind of small, negligible curiosities just about everyone has in their life, the kind that are then mythologized, in hindsight, when the protagonist has become a star in some field. At least that's what people thought until 2017, when an art gallery (the United Talent Agency) hung the first show of artwork by the singer of Nirvana at the Seattle Art Fair. They depicted a "distorted expressionist figure that can be connected to the work of Edvard Munch" (*New York Times*).

Among those images, at least one is well-known to rock fans, because it's the drawing that then became the cover of *Incesticide*, the compilation of singles, demos and covers of Devo and the Vaselines, released by DGC Records in 1992. The image is of a humanoid, skeletal creature being pulled by its (very long) arm by a sort of doll whose head has been bashed open. In the foreground is a red poppy, probably a metaphor for the singer's heroin addiction. The creature seems to be a twin of the other unsettling subject, *Fistula*, exhibited in the same show. Various pages of notes taken from Cobain's diaries were also on display, containing an early draft of the future hit "Smells Like Teen Spirit," a letter in which the singer swore eternal faithfulness to Courtney Love, and a collaboration with writer William S. Burroughs, a pillar of the Beat Generation and Cobain's "toxic idol."

Up until 2017, the year of the art exhibition, Cobain had appeared in three different auctions (Christie's in 2004, Phillips in 2009 and Julien's in 2017), with six pieces in total. Considering the work sold at auction, we can say that those painterly inclinations weren't just the childhood musings of a future pop star, but that Cobain asserted himself in his own way even in the art market, setting the personal record that year, with a 4 x 5½ in (10 × 14 cm) watercolor that went for $64,000. Who knows if he would have been able to continue to develop his artistic talent.

Talent that instead was relegated to the shadows, even in the superstardom that in just a few years would smile upon that shy, slightly melancholy blond young man, with a face so scruffy that even fame didn't seem to seek it out. Yet arrive it did, screeching in on a guitar, instead of on the rustle of brushstrokes.

The family confusion would be clarified on June 28, 1979, when Kurt's mother granted full custody of the twelve-year-old to his father. But things didn't get much better and Kurt began to increasingly stress that they "weren't his real family," perhaps jealous of the attention that he was no longer receiving. However, it was no small trauma, if we are to believe what Cobain wrote in his diary: "The first seven years of my life were exceptional, incredible, realistic...an absolute joy." Then darkness set in, never to truly go away.

Not finding peace in his family life, young Kurt sought out peace elsewhere and, for a short period of time, he even found religion. He became a devout Christian and regularly attended church functions in the neighborhood, but peace still seemed far away, in part because stability at home wasn't guaranteed: for a short period, Donald even entrusted him to the care of the family of his friends, the Reeds, whose son Jesse went to school with Kurt and who was (and would remain to the very end) one of his best friends. Jesse's parents, Ethel and Dave Reed, were born-again Christians, members of Central Park Baptist Church, the church that young Kurt began to attend, both for its functions and for the Christian youth group meetings. His interest in religion didn't last long, even if we can find echoes of the religious experience in some of the songs that he would write in the future, even if a spiritual, interior quest would in any case mark the rest of his growth.

2

1984–1986
MUSIC, PUNK
& LOVE

AT LAST, A NEW WORLD,
ONE THAT ABOUNDED
WITH DREAMS AND SOUNDS

but let's get back to the music. Luckily, as was already mentioned, musical training and stimuli weren't lacking in little Kurt's life, despite the various hardships. Again, his guitaris aunt Mari is the one to inform us that the boy was well fed on rock and pop music. It would be too unreliable to draw hasty conclusions from the sparse notes in family memories but perhaps this is exactly where he got the idea to combine the sonorous assault o punk with decisively pop melodies. In short, it would be the musical mark that would distinguish Nirvana from the sludge of all the other indie bands in the grunge brood.

At the time, Kurt's favorite thing to do was watch television. As Andrea Prevignano has pointed out, "In the States in 1981, the average number of television sets per house was .84, which were in operation an average of five and a half hours per day.

The electronic babysitter would become a veritable backdrop to his afternoons Kurt wasn't just a hyperactive boy with a pronounced sensibility for drawing and music He also was tender at heart and was fascinated by shows about children: he adored *Family Affair* and *The Brady Bunch*, and he was a fan of the story of Jem and Scout, the children of the lawyer Atticus Finch in the beautiful, touching novel *To Kill a Mockingbird* by Harpe Lee on racial segregation in a small town in 1930s Alabama. He was hypnotized in fron of the screen, inhaling science fiction classics such as *Close Encounters of the Third Kind* and *The War of the Worlds*. He had fun watching old episodes of *The A-Team*, but he was thunderstruck by the perverse performance of Jack Nicholson in Stanley Kubrick's

The Shining. MTV had begun broadcasting and became an essential companion to many of his afternoons.

He digested reruns of *The Andy Griffith Show*, a sitcom from the 1960s, stealing ideas from it that he would later use to create a serial killer, the fun Floyd in "Floyd the Barber" (on the debut album *Bleach*).

Once Kurt discovered he enjoyed writing, he began to fill journals with ideas, thoughts and drawings

He began journaling, alternating stories, thoughts and drawings. Up until then, the idea of writing something hadn't even come to mind: "I hadn't ever seriously considered the idea of keeping a journal," Cobain stated. "I hadn't even ever tried to write stories or poetry, and in any case, when I started, it was really abstract stuff. I liked drawing and painting much more, in addition to playing music. But, one thing was certain, it was clear to me that I wanted to be an artist. My mother really supported me in that, she always complimented my drawings, she pushed me to keep going. At school, I had three different art classes and I planned to enroll in art school. But I knew my limits, beyond the nice things they told me." His journals would become important and, after his death, more than twenty notebooks full of texts, drawings, ideas and stories were found, compiled from when he was fourteen up until his final days.

Another important thing happened in 1981: Cobain received a gift from his uncle Chuck. It was his first electric guitar, a Univox Hi-Flier, and an amplifier. The present was greatly appreciated, and Cobain immediately started practicing on the six strings, quickly learning to strum a few hard rock classics. Being ambidextrous, he decided to play left-handed just for the sake of being different. Plus, despite liking the sound of the great hard rock bands of the 1970s, he couldn't stand the machismo. Indeed, Cobain was hardly a "school bully," like some of his attitudes hinted at earlier might lead one to believe (his roughest behavior was reserved for his family). More than anything, he tended to solitude. He hardly had any friends at Weatherwax High School in Aberdeen, where he had enrolled in the meantime. One of those friends was Myer Loftin, an openly gay teen, something that isolated him even more from the rest of their peers, who didn't associate with homosexuals. Actually, Cobain was almost happy for others to think he was gay, because it meant he could live without having to deal too much with others. "I even thought I was gay... although I never experimented with it," Cobain once affirmed in an interview with Jon Savage. "I thought that might be the solution to my problems. Nobody liked me, essentially everyone else was scared of me, but when I started hanging out with that kid, Myer Loftin, who everyone knew was gay, they began mistreating me and they tried to beat me up.

So, my mother intervened and wouldn't let me be friends with him anymore...It was devastating, because finally I'd found a male friend who I actually hugged and could show affection to, and I was told I couldn't spend any more time with him." Back then, he lost a friend but also made two new ones that would be fundamental, destined to shape him for the rest of his short life: the first was the guitar given to him by his uncle Chuck, who in the meantime had gone from the Beachcombers to a local band with a bit of success named Fat Chance. Cobain set into learning how to play, and he loved to invent new melodies, covering any song that came to mind. He spent a lot of time practicing, and it became a sort of obsession, as he himself recounted: "A sort of daily job, even if it wasn't." To improve even more, he asked for a hand from a friend of his uncle, Fat Chance guitarist Warren Mason. Mason helped Cobain get familiar with the instrument, appreciating his passion, dedication and the attention he paid to tiny details. He wasn't particularly technical in his playing and he was far from a "guitar hero," but Cobain immediately showed great concern for what did or did not count within the songs, for their structure, for the sequence of chords. He rarely played in front of others. The other "friendship" that he gained was that with marijuana, which he began to smoke constantly. It was a drug that, despite calming him down, he used to escape reality.

COBAIN'S UNCLE CHUCK GAVE HIM
A GUITAR AND THINGS SUDDENLY
BECAME CLEAR. MUSIC GAVE HIM
A VOICE AND THE INSTRUMENT
BECAME HIS BEST FRIEND

In 1983, Cobain moved back to Aberdeen to live with his mother and her second husband, Pat O'Connor, but the relationship between the two didn't improve very much. He enrolled in Aberdeen High School, which proved to be practically pointless. Two weeks before graduation, he dropped out of high school realizing he didn't have enough credits to graduate and very little desire to study. At that point, his mother gave him an ultimatum: find a job or get out. Cobain stalled; he didn't want to have to choose at all, and he didn't want to go live alone.

So, his mother chose for him, and after a week he found all his belongings packed and ready to go. His new life was about to begin, with no family, no clear idea of what his future held. But at least it was all in his hands; it no longer depended on the decisions of anyone else. However, it wasn't a very pleasant state of things, and Cobain felt abandoned by what had remained standing of his family. He began to live like a vagabond, sometimes crashing at friends' houses, going back to his mother's basement every so often, while legend has it that he even slept under a bridge of the Wishkah River.

Before this big life change, however, Cobain went to his first rock concerts: that of Sammy Hagar (famously known for having replaced David Lee Roth in Van Halen from 1985 to 1996) and that of Quarterflash (mainly known for the record-breaking 1981 single titled "Harden My Heart"), confirming his propensity towards hard rock and catchy pop in equal doses.

He began to explore the music scene in Aberdeen, and after having seen him play live, he got to know Matt Lukin, who was part of a local band, the Melvins. It was Lukin who introduced Cobain to Roger "Buzz" Osborne, the singer and guitarist of the Melvins, and both members of the band would become his friends.

In 1984, the Melvins had just started their career, and they can be rightly considered the pioneers of the grunge scene (even if their first album came out only in 1986), thanks to their torrential discography and their slow, heavy sound (called "sludge metal"), which immensely influenced not just Nirvana but also their peers Soundgarden, Mudhoney and the entire stoner scene. Heavy, but no strangers to points of experimentalism that bordered on noise. It was thus "King Buzzo" that ferried Cobain into the American hardcore punk scene, getting him to listen to its main bands, from Bad Brains to Black Flag, down on to Butthole Surfers and Beat Happening. "My first exposure to punk rock came when *Creem* started covering the Sex Pistols' U.S. tour," Cobain once said. "But I was just eleven years old, and I couldn't possibly have followed them on the tour. The thought of just going to Seattle, which was only 200 miles away was impossible...My aunts would give me Beatles records, so for the most part it was just the Beatles, and every once in a while, if I was lucky, I was able to buy a single. After that, I was always trying to find punk rock, but of course they didn't have it in our record shop in Aberdeen...that stuff finally leaked into Aberdeen many years after the fact... Then, finally, in 1984 a friend of mine named Buzz Osborne made me a couple of compilation tapes...everything, all the most popular punk rock bands, and I was completely blown away. I'd finally found my calling. Punk expressed the way I felt socially and politically...It expressed the anger that I felt, the alienation."

Discovering rock was fundamental. A sound that could express his rage and emotions.

In short, Cobain found a sound that resonated more with his feelings, even if he would always distance himself from the radical stringency of straight edge punk purists, which he thought was a sort of reverse elitism.

So, American punk more than the English variety: as history would have it, the first album by the Ramones came out in April 1976 and, even if the New York "siblings"—Joey, Dee Dee, Johnny and Tommy—still had long hair, blue jeans and leather jackets, their punk attitude arose a full year ahead of the wildly famous exploit that was *Never Mind the Bollocks, Here's the Sex Pistols*. That first and only album by the Sex Pistols would definitively codify the genre, turning them into the undisputed standard bearers. So, if we can agree to consider the New York Dolls (New Yorkers whose self-titled debut album came out in 1973 and the collaboration with Malcolm McLaren in 1975) and Patti Smith (a New Yorker by choice, with *Horses* in 1974) to be the noble precursors of punk, we'd have to conclude that punk was an American music trend, or better yet, specifically from the Big Apple, upon which the English were able to fine-tune and build an enormous phenomenon, a subculture and even "filthy lucre" (as the Sex Pistols themselves defined it) of planetary proportions.

But, if we dig a bit below the surface, we'll discover that essentially stars-and-stripes punk wasn't even entirely concentrated in New York, though we won't rewind the tape of time back to old-timers like the Stooges and MC5 in Detroit. However, it is certain that the English punk of 1977 was the spark that lit the fire of the important Californian punk scene, which came up from the gutters of Los Angeles and San Francisco in the early 1980s. In the case of the former: the Cramps, X, the Gun Club and most importantly the short and turbulent career of the Germs, prematurely cut short after the death by overdose of lead singer Darby Crash, though the band's guitar player Pat Smear would join Nirvana in 1993. And then there's hardcore punk, which took aim at the heart of the "American system" with sarcasm, anarchy and political messages, with bands like the habitual offenders from San Francisco the Dead Kennedys, led by Jello Biafra, and Black Flag with Henry Rollins and Greg Ginn, on up to Minor Threat. The fusion of punk rage and slower, heavier rhythms—characteristic of hard rock from the 1970s (Black Sabbath first and foremost) and even more so of the subsequent heavy metal of Iron Maiden, Motörhead and later Metallica—is probably the key to understanding the sound that would come into its own in Seattle, called grunge by the founders of the soon-to-be iconic label Sub Pop, of which Nirvana was the juiciest fruit.

A detail from the cover of a cassette tape by Fecal Matter, 1985.

But let's get back to young Kurt: Buzz Osborne gave his confidence a boost, telling him that he should leave the small world of Aberdeen behind and start looking more assuredly towards Seattle, certain of his musical talent. In addition to expanding Kurt's musical horizons, he also introduced him to lots of other young musicians in the area. Kurt was in a truly dark place, without a place to live, already using drugs regularly, without any real prospects. Suddenly, however, he decided to "get serious" about music, the only thing that truly interested him. He got his first band, Fecal Matter, together in 1985, just after having dropped out of Aberdeen High School, one of the many groups that had sprung up around the "success" of the Melvins. It was a trio, with Cobain on guitar, Greg Hokanson on drums and Dale Crover, the bassist from the Melvins, well, on bass. Their set list was made up of covers, mainly punk and hard rock. Nothing overwhelming, but just enough to start to pave a path, to make sense of the nothing that until that moment seemed to surround his existence, and a way to start writing something. Finally, music was at the center of it all. In the creation of the group, a friend that Kurt had met in the rehearsal studio of the Melvins played a fundamental role: Krist Novoselic. Two years older than Kurt but, like him, essentially a dropout with similar taste in music. Novoselic's mom had a beauty shop in the city, with a basement that she generously let her son and his friends use for band practice. And that is precisely where Fecal Matter was born. But perhaps more importantly, it's where the friendship between Kurt and Krist solidified. However, it was over in the house of his Aunt Mari that Kurt and Crover recorded their first demo, on a four-track tape recorder, between late 1985 and early 1986. With Crover on bass and drums, they captured 13 tracks that, as Cobain would later say, reflected his passion

for Black Sabbath and Black Flag. The title of the recordings was decidedly ironic, *Illiteracy Will Prevail*, and the content was decidedly varied in its themes. Some of the songs they recorded would eventually see the light of day, including "Downer," which was included on *Bleach*, the debut album of Nirvana, and "Spank Thru," which was released in 1988 on *Sub Pop 200*, a compilation that presented the Seattle grunge scene. Even Buzz Osborne and the drummer from the Melvins, Mike Dillard, shortly joined the group, which played live just once, on May 3, 1986, in Olympia, under the name Brown Towel. Then the group broke up and Novoselic joined Cobain to form a band whose name changed more than once (among the more creative monikers, the Sellouts and the Stiff Woodies), as did its members, which included Steve Newman and Bob McFadden. That all changed in early 1987, when the two met Aaron Burckhard, who would officially join as the drummer. Seattle was almost within reach.

BEFORE MOVING TO SEATTLE, COBAIN LIVED IN OLYMPIA, WHERE HE PLAYED IN SMALL CLUBS, WROTE MUSIC AND, FOR THE FIRST TIME, FOUND LOVE

But let's not get ahead of ourselves: in late 1986, Cobain was still a hair from homelessness. He managed to snag an apartment, paying rent with money he made working at the Polynesian Resort, a Pacific-themed hotel in Ocean Shores, Washington, just under 20 miles (30 km) west of Aberdeen. However, the goal remained the one pinpointed by Osborne: making it to Seattle. But in between, there was another city, Olympia, where the music scene was more vibrant and interesting and where Cobain had made his first appearance on stage. There he would play again, at small concerts and house parties, nothing big, but just enough to make him feel able to keep going onwards and upwards. And, most importantly, to try to play not just the usual covers, but also the first songs he had started to write. And Olympia, in 1987, is where he found love. It was no small thing, far from it. Until then, Cobain hadn't had a real girlfriend. He was shy, girls liked him, but he was unable to be relaxed and to be himself, to let go, around anyone of the opposite sex. Doing a bit of research, it seems that his first "love" was Roni Toyra in Montesano when he was twelve, and his first kiss was probably with Andrea Vance, again in Montesano, at sixteen. In his journals, a more troubling story appears, that of a short encounter, heavy petting, with a girl with psychological issues in the summer of 1983 in Aberdeen, which ended in a police investigation after the girl told her father about it. But in reality, no one in

Aberdeen had ever heard of such a story and no matches are to be found. To the contrary: all his

friends and acquaintances from that time deny ever hearing of such a thing, and in a small town,

word would have easily spread in the face of such an event. In any case, Cobain wrote it in his

journal, though it is also worth mentioning that the same journal contains lots of other invented

stories and even lots of "friends" that never actually existed. In any case, Cobain's first "real"

girlfriend was Jackie Hagara, in Aberdeen. But even here, the whole story is a bit fuzzy. Some say

the two were together between the fall of 1983 and April of 1984, while others insist they were just

close friends and when the thing was about to get serious, her mother stepped in to put an end to

it. Legend has it that when Jackie's mother broke them up, Cobain ended up losing his virginity to

one of Jackie's friends. So, when he got together with Tracy Marander, we can say that it was the

first time that Cobain had a serious girlfriend. A girl who didn't just love him, but who believed in

him and supported him. Cobain ended up going to live with her (she worked at a coffee shop in the

airport), but his lifestyle didn't change. He continued to be erratic, and he basically stayed home

all day, except for when he left to play with the band, writing and testing songs out. At home, he

would watch television, read, use soft drugs, take care of small animals and dream. But Cobain

increasingly wanted his musician dream to become reality, and to do so, to be able to record a demo

of the songs he was writing in a real studio, he needed money.

He finally found a job as a janitor and he began setting aside his earnings. Given that, we can't say that his life revolved around love, because, in truth, it only revolved around music. But the desire to have stable emotional relationships, in contrast to the family chaos that had so bothered him up until then, was strong. The only thing stronger than love was his drive to make it to Seattle and record his music. But to do so, he would still have to enrich his personal experience, both in emotional terms (and in this area his relationship with Tracy Marander was important) and in cultural terms. In reality, Cobain had always loved reading: "As a boy, I read everything that I could get my hands on. I went to the library a lot, especially when I skipped school, both in junior high and high school," Cobain once said. "It was the only place I could go. I didn't know what to read, so I'd pick books randomly. But I'd also read a lot when I went to school, because it allowed me to isolate myself and not talk to others. Sometimes I'd even pretend to read so that people wouldn't bother me." "Despite cathodic overexposure," explained Andrea Prevignano, "Cobain created his own intellectual path."

He rejected the education that was imposed upon him, but he gravitated around school, even when it seemed he had abandoned it. In Aberdeen, he often went to Timberland Library, at 121 East Market Street, where he'd keep himself entertained for hours, scouring through contemporary American literature and searching for music business manuals. And even when he began hanging out in Olympia around 20 years old, the university town was the destination of his wanderings, and it was the cultured and rebellious young people of the local indie rock scene that most interested him. One book in particular won him over: *All You Need to Know About the Music Business* by Donald Passman. He spent his teen years listening to the Beatles and Lennon, one of his greatest, and never admitted, passions, and watching the favorite cult film of every young aspiring axe hero, *This Is Spinal Tap*. He turned the pages of *Sex Pistols*, the

COBAIN READ A LOT OF BOOKS, WATCHED A LOT OF TV AND BEGAN EXPERIMENTING WITH DIFFERENT DRUGS

illustrated biography of the British punk band written by Fred and Judy Vermorel. He bought or borrowed industry magazines and fanzines like the punk bible *Maximum Rocknroll*, *Backlash* and *The Rocket*. He found old issues of *Creem* from the 1970s and he avidly read all that was written by Lester Bangs, the most famous, talented and tragic of all American music critics. He read the local press and at times he even was inspired by it. From the headlines of newspapers displayed in drugstores, he learned of the story of the girl kidnapped on her way back from a punk concert and tortured. The story ended up in "Polly" (on *Nevermind*), a chilling tale of psychological violence narrated by the distressed perspective of the tormenter. In short, he was curious; he wasn't apathetic or superficial. He had his own way of seeing reality and of establishing personal relationships. It wasn't easy to become part of his universe, and for Tracy in particular, it was especially hard. But their relationship went on, despite the challenges and despite the increasing use of alcohol and drugs. Not just marijuana, but also heavier drugs, of all types, "practically every type of drug in existence," he would later say in an interview. Some drugs, especially painkillers that cause addiction, were prescribed to Cobain to help reduce his constant stomach pain. But his familiarity with just about every substance there is led him to the use of heavy drugs, such as cocaine and heroin. Self-destructive? According to him, no. Actually, the idea of ending up like rockstars who died young wasn't his style, as he dreamed of being a success, of being able to play and live a better life, different from the life he wanted to leave behind.

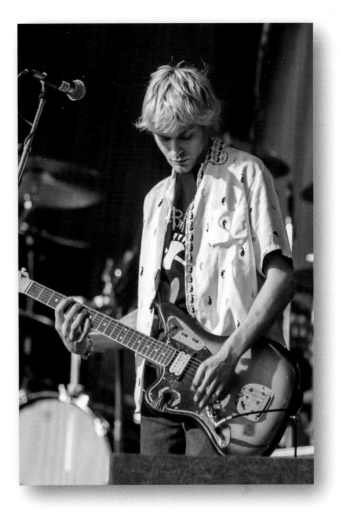

Cobain on stage at Kalvøyafestivalen, in Norway, in the summer of 1992.

SEATTLE

For Cobain and his band, the goal, it bears repeating, was Seattle. But why Seattle? Why did that rainy port city in the State of Washington (the rainiest, it seems, and the most "cultured" of all American cities based on the number of libraries and college graduates per capita) become the center of the raging music scene now universally known as grunge? After all, it's certainly a "calmer" city than New York and Los Angeles, or even Chicago and Detroit. Despite having a solid musical past (the jazz scene dates back to the Roaring '20s), Seattle, as we have already noted, is a bit provincial in terms of rock history.

It's true that it's the hometown of Jimi Hendrix, but the great Black guitarist gained fame in London before his birthplace; after his electric arc forever changed the history of electric guitars and music in general, the city wasn't pervaded by other high-tension shocks, despite having baptized the career of Heart, a strange lineup in the early 1970s. They were pioneers in the fusion of hard rock, proto metal and even folk, and trailblazers of co-ed band formations, with a female singer (Ann Wilson) and a female guitarist (Nancy Wilson) (the two are sisters), accompanied by a quartet of male musicians. Then, in the early 1980s, the city gave us Queensrÿche, the band that paved the way for progressive metal, and creators of the highly praised Orwellian concept album *Operation: Mindcrime*, released in 1988.

Few tracks, in short, but all in the sign of cross-pollination between hard rock and other sonic spices. Sure, it was easy for the din of the hardcore punk scene of faraway Washington, D.C., to be carried on the cold wind of the northwest even to rainy Seattle, but in any case, in 1989, the clanking motor of grunge was already in motion: Soundgarden had made their debut in 1987 with their *Screaming Life* EP, and by 1988, they were already on their first monumental album (*Ultramega OK*); Green River had put out their one and only album (*Rehab Doll*) in 1988; Mudhoney, with Mark Arm and Steve Turner, began their career in 1989 with the *Superfuzz Bigmuff* EP.

All of them, of course, were put out by Sub Pop, the label that defined the sound of the Pacific Northwest.

The stew had been simmering in the Sub Pop pot since the *Sub Pop 100* compilation released in 1986,

in which none of the stars of the grunge scene yet appeared, though their inspiration Steve Albini (singer-guitarist of Big Black, later the producer of the Pixies and Nirvana's *In Utero*), Sonic Youth and Savage Republic did, just to name a few. Since the fuse had already been lit, Kurt couldn't wait to follow the flame: with the money he had saved up from work, and after having parted ways with Aaron Burckhard, Kurt and Krist once again called Dale Crover and, in January 1988, finally rented a recording studio in Seattle to put their music in demo form. It all happened at Reciprocal Recordings, run by Jack Endino, who played in Skin Yard but who also rented out space in his studio to all the best bands in the scene.

They recorded ten songs in just a few hours, as they had to finish in time to reach Tacoma, about 40 miles (65 kilometers) from Seattle, where they had been booked for a concert—the only official concert that Cobain and Novoselic would play with Dale Crover. Endino and the band spent five hours recording, "about six minutes per song," remembered Endino. What once seemed like a dream was finally taking shape.

3

1987–1990
NIRVANA:
FROM THE BASEMENT
TO *NEVERMIND*

SEATTLE, GRUNGE
AND THE WORLD'S MOST
POPULAR ROCK TRIO

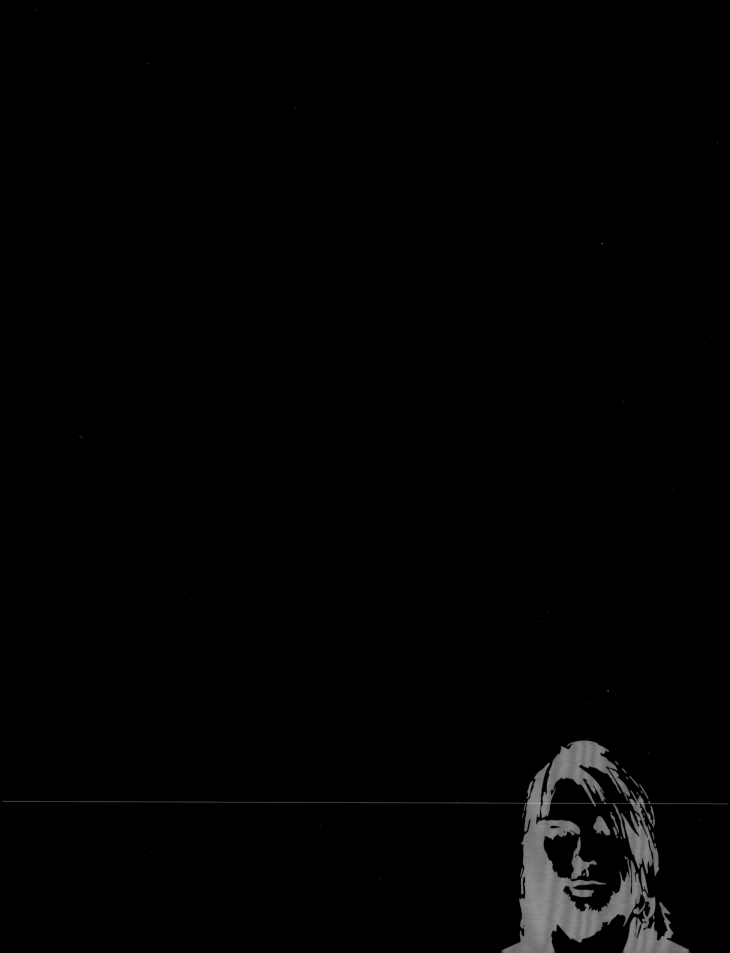

The founding nucleus of Nirvana was the Kurt Cobain-Krist Novoselic duo. At a towering six feet seven inches (2.01 meters), Krist Anthony Novoselic is one of the tallest living musicians in the world, today a nice, balding fifty-eight-year-old and father of two children with his wife, artist Darbury Ayn Stenderu. Krist was born on May 16, 1965, in Compton, California, to Marija and Kristo Novoselic, Croatian immigrants who had moved from Zadar to the West Coast. They called Aberdeen home as of 1979, landing in a vibrant Croatian community. But in order to get established and have less trouble, they sent young Krist to Croatia the following year, though he was back stateside by 1981. His little brother, Robert, was the one who introduced him to Cobain, and the two bonded over a shared passion for punk rock.

THE FIRST CONCERT AS NIRVANA WAS HELD IN LATE MAY 1988

From that moment on, the two were always together. But the third element of the first incarnation of Nirvana was Chad Channing, a peer of Kurt's and a drummer who had already played with a few other bands in the area (with musicians that would pave the way, like Jason Everman and Ben Shepherd). A mutual friend introduced him to Kurt and to Krist, and after a few practices together, the three became a band. They had already been going by the name Nirvana for a few months, since March 1988, but the first concert together with the official moniker was in late May of that same year.

But how did they manage to put out their first single, how did Kurt Cobain actually manage to physically create a small vinyl disc, how did he make his dream come true? Let's go a few months back in time. Once the demo was recorded in January 1988, Cobain began carrying it around with him, having anyone who was interested give it a listen. But Jack Endino, who had been positively impressed by the energy and the feeling of the band, went one step further: he took it to Jonathan Poneman, who worked with Bruce Pavitt and his independent record label, Sub Pop.

Pavitt had founded the label in Olympia in 1979, first as a fanzine, which in its short lifespan (just nine issues) adopted the strategy of alternating paper issues with cassette tape compilations of indie bands. After issue nine, they would become a series of underground rock tapes. The cassette series also came to an end shortly afterwards, and Pavitt moved to Seattle, opening a record store called Fallout Records, and simultaneously writing a "Sub Pop U.S.A." column in the bi-weekly music magazine *The Rocket* and hosting a show on KCMU, a local FM radio station dedicated to indie rock. The year 1986 was the official launch: the *Sub Pop 100* compilation was released,

exploring all the subgenres of alternative rock at the time, destined to become a point of reference for the grunge to come. Kim Thayil, guitarist of Soundgarden, introduced Pavitt to the young Poneman, who had funded the recording of the band's first single, impressed by Chris Cornell's voice. The two decided to set up a true record label, and that label was Sub Pop. The next year, the first EP by Green River came out, *Dry as a Bone*, launched as "ultra-loose grunge that destroyed the morals of a generation." It was the birth of grunge, the dawn of a new sound that would change the world shortly after, leaving an undying echo in its wake. Soundgarden's *Hunted Down/ Nothing to Say* (the A and B sides of the single) came out in July 1987, then it was the turn of Mudhoney, with 800 copies of the *Touch Me I'm Sick* single.

Endino gave Nirvana's demo to Poneman, who had Pavitt listen to it. "It was early 1988," remembered Pavitt. "I listened to it and I thought it was interesting, with great potential. It was definitely different than the others, but it was especially clear that Cobain had an incredible voice." In April, Nirvana played for the first time in Seattle, at the Central Saloon, in a sort of showcase precisely for the heads of Sub Pop. "No one came," explained Pavitt. "But, listening to the entire set, there was a song that came out great, 'Love Buzz,' and it was a cover. But it showed the road that the band was heading down, both in the hypnotic arrangement, and in how it was tied to Cobain's writing style."

Krist Novoselic on stage at the Palatrussardi arena in Milan, February 25, 1994.

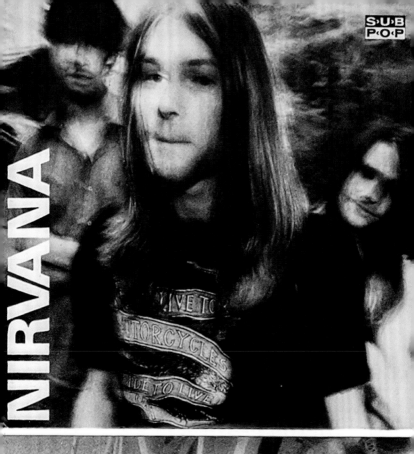

SUB POP

NIRVANA

LOVE BUZZ
b/w
BIG CHEESE

KURDT KOBAIN:
VOCALS, GUITAR
CHRIS NOVOSELIC:
BASS
CHAD CHANNING:
DRUMS

RECORDED AT RECIPROCAL STUDIOS,
SEATTLE. PRODUCED BY JACK EN-
DINO & NIRVANA.

PHOTOGRAPHS BY ALICE WHEELER.
INNER LABEL DESIGN BY SUSANNE SASIC.
JACKET DESIGN BY LISA ORTH.
LOVE BUZZ WRITTEN BY ROBBY VAN LEEUWEN.

764 /1000

The song was a Shocking Blue cover, a Dutch band that had brought "Venus" to international success in 1969. Unlike "Venus," when the original "Love Buzz" was released in 1967, it was a bit of a flop. But Novoselic really loved the track and had convinced Cobain to make a version of it. At first, Cobain agreed just to please his friend, who had discovered the album by the Dutch band by chance in a used record shop. Cobain didn't much care for music with psychedelic flair, but he slowly began to appreciate the track and had fun singing it. After the concert, Pavitt and Poneman decided to meet Cobain. After setting up a meeting in a café in Seattle's Capitol Hill district, Pavitt was convinced, Poneman got Nirvana under contract, and Cobain could finally record their first single, with production entrusted to Endino once again at his cramped Reciprocal Recording studios. The single, recorded on June 11, 1988, was printed with just 1,000 copies and distributed in November of that same year by pre-order exclusively to the 2,000 members of the Sub Pop "Singles Club," a service that was inaugurated by Nirvana themselves. "We had released a single, but no one could buy it," Novoselic explained, but the strategy of Poneman and Pavitt was a success, because in addition to being "sold out," it also quickly generated hype and curiosity around the band. Cobain was the one to then light the fuse: once the single had come out, he expected it to become part of the regular rotation on the college radio station that was dialed into everything up-and-coming, KCMU, but he never heard the song on the air, despite having the radio constantly on at home and in the car. He then had an idea: he went out in search of a payphone, inserted a coin and called the radio station, asking them to play "Love Buzz," the new Nirvana single. A few minutes later, they did just that and the song aired on the radio, marking the first time in Cobain's life that he got to listen to his music on the airwaves. It's hard to say how much this thrilled him, but we can certainly imagine that everything he had dreamed of was wrapped up in those 3:34 minutes in which he was silent, listening to his music as it came out of the radio.

The front and back covers of the first Nirvana single, "Love Buzz," released on November 1, 1988.

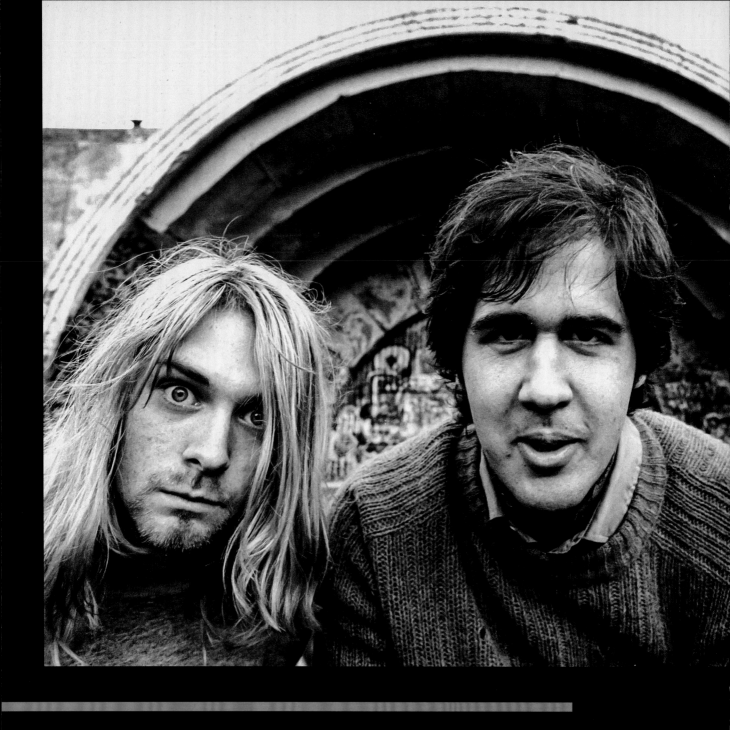

A picture of Nirvana taken in April 1990 in New York. From left: Kurt Cobain, Krist Novoselic and Chad Channing.

It was the start of a new life for Cobain, the life that he had always wanted. Sure, it wasn't exactly the one he had dreamed of. The crowds at the band's concerts weren't exactly large, their music was still taking shape, and the ideas he had in mind hadn't quite come into sharp focus, but everything was moving in the right direction, even in terms of love. Though it must be said that Cobain's world was still more grey than colorful, as depression was always around the corner. A bad day was all it might take to derail the new train, and his drug use (even if he was convinced he could keep it under control) certainly didn't help to completely "brighten" a life that in many ways seemed like it was improving. And able to improve even more. Because in any case, the band worked, because the concerts were multiplying, because the god of creativity had offered to help him and the new, strange, unhinged, powerful, passionate songs followed him everywhere and he captured them, he took them and shaped them. He had found a way to express his interior world, he had found a way to crush his demons. Not always, and not all of them. But what he was doing was enough to convince Sub Pop to put Nirvana to work on the creation of an album. Actually, Sub Pop just wanted to record an EP. It would have been good enough just to put Nirvana's music out there, and to Cobain it was better than good, it was already a great achievement. The three bandmates got to work, and for a few weeks in October, they tried out the tracks they already had in their repertoire and added a few of Cobain's new compositions. Then they once again headed to Endino's Reciprocal Recordings and got to work, on December 24, 1988, Christmas Eve, for a five-hour session. This was followed by a few days off, in which Cobain wrote a letter to his grandparents: "Dear long-lost grandparents, I miss you very much, which is no excuse for my not visiting. I'm very busy living in Olympia when I'm not on tour with my band. We've put out a single just recently and it has sold out already. We are recording for our debut LP this Monday which will be released in March. In February we are going on tour again

Bleach wasn't an EP, but a full album. It was recorded in about 30 hours and included the tracks recorded previously with Endino. The first session, as we said, was on Christmas Eve, then again between December 29 and 31, and then on January 14 and 24 of the new year. Despite Chad Channing joining the band, three songs ("Floyd the Barber," "Paper Cuts" and "Downer") still came from the recordings with Dale Crover. All combined, there were 11 tracks for just 37 minutes and 19 seconds of play time, which was all it took to make a permanent mark on rock history: clanking and noisy, spartanly produced by Endino, no-frills, in-line with the more "official" grunge coordinates, not so much as a hint of the physical absence of the second guitar, credited to Jason Everman in the liner notes (he hadn't so much as played a note, or close to it, during the recording session). Yet he played a fundamental role in the creation of the album because he was the one who paid the $606.17 that those recordings cost. Everman, born in Alaska in 1967, the same year as Cobain, was thus added to the credits of *Bleach* out of gratitude. Shortly after, he drifted away from the band because his tastes were tending more towards heavy metal than the other members of Nirvana. And they had very different tastes, since, as Novoselic recalled, on their way to record the

The first songs written by Cobain were a combination of hard rock and melodies, punk and tenderness

album they listened to the music of the Smithereens and Celtic Frost, just to explain the extremes between which their sonic universe oscillated: melodyand metal nihilism. Cobain recounted that some of the lyrics were written the night before leaving for Seattle, and others while they were in the car heading to the studio. Cobain never paid particular attention to the lyrics, what he cared about was the words having a certain sound, and that sound had to go well with his voice. He even said it in one of his earliest interviews: "When I write a song, the lyrics are the last thing I think about. I can go from two or three subjects in a track and the title might not have any meaning. Sometimes I try to do things that are more difficult, just to make myself feel a bit angrier, I create conflicts like fights with other people." Stuff he invented, essentially, not necessarily experienced or true. "I limit myself to yelling out negative lyrics, as long as they aren't sexist and they don't make me feel ashamed. None of these lyrics are dear to me."

The cover of Bleach *by Nirvana, released by Sub Pop in 1989.*

They're lyrics that are bitter and at times senseless, they play upon sounds and despair and they're just autobiographical enough, as is clear in "School" or "Blew," about living in a small and small-minded town like Aberdeen. But they're powerful, with a pulsating bass intro and a clear punk-style single-note riff, which also recurs in "Floyd the Barber," a barber that the songwriter imagines being tortured by, inspired by *The Andy Griffith Show* (which was playing on the TV the day Cobain's body was found). It's hard not to see similarities with Cobain, even in the antisocial, drugged up, "negative and disgusting" guy in "Negative Creep," while the tense "Paper Cuts" is an ode to their musical godfathers, the Melvins, with its heavy cement riff, the only song in which the word "Nirvana" appears: Cobain sings from the point of view of two kids locked in the attic by their parents (a real event that made the news in Aberdeen). These tracks, along with the cover of Shocking Blue's "Love Buzz" immediately established the parameters of the Nirvana sound. A rough, cantankerous sound that mixes the dirty blues rock of the Rolling Stones and the Stooges with the power of hard rock (Led Zeppelin to Aerosmith), and with the hardcore fervor of Hüsker Dü and the Pixies. And then the ultra-hard "Scoff," "Swap Meet" and "Mr. Moustache," which pays distant homage to the Doors' "Hello, I Love You" riff to satirize the figure of a muscular macho

redneck. "So primitive that they manage to make label mates Mudhoney sound like Genesis" (as described by *NME*), putting it bluntly. *Bleach* delivered Nirvana's style to the plates of record players in a one-two punch: simple motifs that were essentially pop, grumbled by Cobain almost as if singing bothered him, up until the explosion of the chorus, which was yelled in a much more acute, biting register. Experts say that if he had lived a long life, singing in that excessive way would have ruined his vocal cords in no time at all. The next (and definitive) drummer, Dave Grohl, later said that even during the production of *Nevermind*, "they could only record one track per day because Kurt lost his voice at the end of every session." Cobain had a range similar to Bob Dylan, far from the five octaves and three notes of his "rival" Axl Rose, though not even with the dramatic and much more shrill high notes of his "grunge peers" Chris Cornell and Layne Staley. "It was like he had nails in his throat," is another way in which Grohl described Cobain's voice, and perhaps those physical limits were what made his rough, scratchy singing a symbol of all of Generation X, that of the 1990s, nerds who were a bit melancholy and introverted who didn't want to grow up, down on the future and unable to articulate a serious ideological rebellion to the establishment in which they found themselves, as their hippy parents did back in 1968.

"Rap music is the only vital form of music introduced since punk rock."

| KURT COBAIN

By whom young Gen Xers in the 1990s felt a bit betrayed. "Only kids and losers know what it means to feel betrayed. Adults, on the other hand, the ones that hold the power, can never hope to understand Nirvana," efficiently summarized Everett True, a writer for *Melody Maker* and later a personal friend of Cobain's and a biographer of Nirvana. The general sound of *Bleach* was in the vein of the original grunge, dirty and loud, where you can't so much as find a trace of a synthesizer, a drum machine, of a sound reworked by a computer, as seemed obligatory in the pop of the 1980s. "That's how Sup Pop wanted it," Cobain said. Because they were the ones reshaping Seattle, transforming it into the capital of rock. Rock has had many capitals: Liverpool, London, New York, San Francisco, Los Angeles, Memphis, Detroit, and even Manchester and Berlin, Paris and Dublin, each with its own bands, style, dreams and fashions. Then Seattle came along, giving us some of the most visible bands from the late 1980s to the early 1990s, the ones that changed the rules of success, bringing the sound of distorted guitars and long messy hair back into the spotlight, for a look that was anything but reassuring. Rock without good manners, light years away from the pop and dance that was at the top of the charts along with the courteous, melodic rock of American superstars. What was coming out of Seattle was rock that ideally was similar to the music of the 1960s and 1970s, but

SOUNDGARDEN, PEARL JAM, TAD, MUDHONEY AND MANY OTHERS WOULD DEFINE THEIR OWN UNIQUE SOUND

also to the violence of metal, which had won over the hearts and minds of the younger generations. This type of rock was labeled "grunge," which was helpful in identifying a number of bands that shared not just a sound, but an attitude, a stance on music. Bands like Nirvana, of course, Soundgarden, Tad, Mudhoney, Pearl Jam and Screaming Trees, just to mention a few, born and raised in the indie market that had Sub Pop at its base, later becoming the spearhead of new American rock. The sound of the bands from Seattle had its roots well planted in the style of punk, with its direct, crude texture, and in the development of an independent record industry done on the cheap, betting it all on the music and change.

The word "grunge" comes from the adjective "grungy," a slang expression in vogue in the 1960s used to indicate someone dirty and grimy. By 1987, it was official: Bruce Pavitt at Sub Pop used "grunge" to promote the second EP by Green River, *Dry as a Bone*. From that moment on, the word was used to label the sound of the bands from Seattle, even if they were quite different from one another.

Naturally, over time, the definition (not unlike what happened with "punk" or "new wave") was overblown and abused by the media, and it was rejected by the stars of the scene as a label that would help sell albums and merch.

Bleach isn't just hard 'n' heavy. It also contains melodic tracks, like "About a Girl," which is about the desire for a friendly relationship with a girl, but "as equals" and also without commitment: it seems to refer to Tracy Marander, who took the picture on the cover of the album.

It seems that this song was written by Cobain after spending an entire afternoon listening to *Meet the Beatles!* on loop (the second album by the Fab Four released in the U.S.). Now a classic in the Nirvana discography, beloved by fans, "About a Girl" got its title by chance. The singer had come into the studio to record it without having one in mind, and when asked what it was about, Cobain responded, "It's about a girl." And the rest is history.

When Nirvana's first album came out, it wasn't a resounding success as far as the charts were concerned. It didn't even make it to being listed. What it did get was some support from college radio stations specializing in alternative music and good reviews from the press. It only sold about 40,000 copies, which wasn't bad for an alt rock album, though still far from a mass culture phenomenon. However, reissued by Geffen after the major-label success of *Nevermind*, the album then sold 1,900,000 copies in the U.S. alone, earning its place as Sub Pop's best-selling album of all time.

While the picture on the cover of *Bleach* (on which even the fleeting Everman appears) was taken by Marander during a concert at the Reko Muse art gallery in Olympia in February 1989, Nirvana would play at different venues on the West Coast, including the University of Washington. From there, to promote the album, on October 23 the group appeared on stage at the Riverside venue in Newcastle upon Tyne, kicking off their first European tour: a double-headliner along with labelmates Tad. On December 3, they played a triumphant set at the London Astoria.

Among the very few that truly had been following the band of Kurt (who, on *Bleach*, even wrote his name as "Kurdt") and Krist, another creative—yet drug-addicted—mind from the grunge scene was at a concert in Kittitas County in Washington State: Mark Lanegan. "Once the three-piece group began playing, however, the wall of noise, the raw catchiness of the songs and the voice of the left-handed guitar-playing singer made me realize I was witnessing something special. Perhaps one of the best bands I'd ever seen," said the then singer of Screaming Trees. "I congratulated Kurt and he did the same with me, declaring himself a fan of Screaming Trees. I walked back to my depressing hovel with an electricity in my step and a newfound buoyancy of spirit. I couldn't shake the notion that I had just experienced something touched by greatness...It had been easy for us to become friends, just a couple of long phone calls talking about girls, music, life. I loved Kurt." The two loved each other enough to immediately start collaborating on music too: in that same year, 1989, "Kurdt" and Krist were in the studio with Lanegan, who was launching his solo career even during the Screaming Trees period with *The Winding Sheet* (also released by Sub Pop), on which Cobain sang "Down in the Dark" and, most notably, the cover of Leadbelly's "Where Did You Sleep Last Night?" which would later be performed by Nirvana on the band's historic unplugged show for MTV, their last official recording.

Unfortunately, even back then, Cobain and his friend Lanegan shared another, more dangerous passion: heroin. In reality, as we said, Cobain had started using marijuana, LSD and psychoactive drugs as a teen, while he began having shooting stomach pains that would last his entire life, "treated" with all the substances he could find. In an interview with *Rolling Stone*, he said that his stomach pain was so bad that it led him to have serious problems with food, until he even developed thoughts of self-harm: "I wanted to kill myself every day. I came very close many times...It was to the point where I was on tour, lying on the floor, vomiting air because I couldn't hold down water." Of course, Cobain went to different doctors, but none of them could find the cause, with hypotheses that ranged from childhood scoliosis to the stress of the rock 'n' roll lifestyle. It seems that just in the last few months of his life, a displaced vertebra had been identified as the source of his pain, benefitting from physiotherapy. Even if by now it was probably too late to "treat" many of his other problems.

The fact is that, afflicted by those gastric pains, chronic bronchitis and probably also undiagnosed bipolar disorder, let down by "official" medicine, Cobain met heroin in 1989 and realized that it was the only substance that managed to completely get rid of his pain. Actually, the first encounter was precisely in the guise of a painkiller, Percodan, a synthetic opium analgesic that a drug dealer had stolen from a pharmacy and sold to Cobain for a dollar, a painkiller

that actually was incredibly addictive, even if Cobain didn't know it back then. When the dealer's Percodan supply ran out, he offered Cobain heroin instead. Sadly, he was hooked in no time. In his journals, he described the start of addiction: "I remember someone saying if you try heroine once you'll become hooked. Of course I laughed and scoffed at the idea but I now believe this to be very true. Not literally, I mean if you do dope once you don't instantly become addicted, it usually takes about one month of everyday use to physically become addicted.

But after the first time your mind say ahh that was very pleasant as long as I don't do it every day, I won't have a problem.

The problem is it happens over time. Let's start with January 1st. Let's do dope for the first time.

Consciously you won't do it again for maybe a month, February you'll do it twice, March 3 days in a row...April 5 days in a row, skip 3 once more. May 10 days in a row. During those ten days it's very easy to lose track of time. It may seem like 3 days but two weeks can go by. The effects are still as pleasant and you can still choose what days you do it so naturally there must not be a problem.

With everyone some time at least once a year some sort of crisis happens to everyone, the loss of a friend or mate or relative this is when the drug tells you to say f**k it. Every drug addict has said f**k it more times than they can count...by the time you've said f**k it the long process of trying to stay off begins."

1990

A photograph of Nirvana taken in London in October 1990. From left: Krist Novoselic, Kurt Cobain and Dave Grohl.

Above and opposite: Nirvana photographed on a roof in London in 1990.

4

1991–1992
SEATTLE:
THE CENTER
OF ROCK

A NEW YOUTH COUNTERCULTURE,
AN AMERICAN
MUSIC REVOLUTION

What was the rock scene like at that time? On the one hand, there was grunge, a form of alternative rock, carried forth mainly by college radio and appreciated by an audience of university students, or at least young people who were "cultured" enough to critique the way of life of the average American and to seek out expression in music that is intentionally rough, dirty and "angry." On the other, there was a "redneck" working class that yearned for the trappings promised by the American dream (success, fame, money), which they didn't even have half a mind to challenge. Despite being those who lost out in Bush's America, the latter class is portrayed to a T in the songs of Bruce Springsteen (who not surprisingly created the title track to *The Wrestler*, which spoke of the similarities between the main character and the actor who played him). So, fans of the "fun, fun, fun" hair metal

COBAIN WANTED TO DISTANCE HIMSELF FROM THE MACHISMO OF AMERICAN ROCK OF THE TIME

that's all hot babes, alcohol binges, motorcycle races and fist fights on Saturday night, the kind of music that's only transgressive in the pirate-like looks of its stars and not much else, the kind that deep down actually embraces the values of the dominant culture and "the system."

This socio-cultural split can even be seen in the tense relationship that Cobain always had with the contemporary champions of the genre, Guns N' Roses, and their frontman Axl Rose in particular, the uncouth and arrogant nemesis of everything that the introverted and reserved Cobain represented in music.

The love story between Kurt Cobain and Tracy Marander ended in 1990; that same year, he entered into a short-lived relationship with someone central to the riot grrl scene, which was flourishing in the Pacific Northwest: Tobi Vail, the drummer of the punk feminist band Bikini Kill. The two met in Olympia, and Cobain immediately found himself at ease with "riotous feminism," given that he did all he could to distance himself from the implicit machismo in the cock rock that he so despised. Later on, Vail admitted to the musical influence of Cobain and, in particular, to having borrowed from him the "scream" that allowed her to use her voice like a musical instrument. The most legendary detail of their flirtation is surely linked to a "riotous" night in which Kathleen Hanna, the lead singer of Bikini Kill, wrote "KURT SMELLS LIKE TEEN SPIRIT" on his bedroom wall. The prank referred to the name of the deodorant used by Vail, though Cobain managed to tease a metaphor out of it.

In September 1990, "Sliver," the last single by Nirvana on Sub Pop, was published. It was recorded once again by Endino at Reciprocal Recordings, during a break in a session by their friends and labelmates Tad, with their instruments and Dan Peters of Mudhoney on drums. The text is about an event in Cobain's childhood in which he was unwillingly left by his parents at his grandparents' house, as his parents wanted to go out and see a show (giving rise to the desperate cry of "Grandma take me home!").

But big changes had already began in the summer of 1990: Dave Grohl was playing drums in a punk band called Scream when Cobain and a few of his friends went to see them perform at a concert in San Francisco. Cobain wasn't happy with Chad Channing; he knew that the band needed a different drummer and he was impressed by Grohl's sound and style. Grohl got an invite and went to the Seattle studio with Kurt and Krist. In the band's biography, Novoselic remembers the moment in which they saw him play: "We knew within two minutes that he was the right drummer. He was a hard hitter. He was really dynamic. He was so bright, so hot, so vital." As Cobain himself once said: "Krist and I have been playing together for about four and a half years now with a few different drummers. And Dave has been in the band for a year. This is the first time we've ever felt like a very definite unit." Grohl immediately got along with the other two, but he also instantly knew that there was something dysfunctional in the trio, something that cut through the soul and mind of Cobain, something intangible and impossible to grasp. Both came from broken homes, but while Cobain grew up with a sense of abandonment, Grohl's mother was present and supportive: "We were young, and the world was just so strange. But that emotional dysfunction in Nirvana was relieved when we put on instruments. If the music hadn't worked, we wouldn't have been there together. I truly believe that there's some people you can only communicate with musically. And sometimes that's an even greater, deeper communication." Using the word "balance" when talking about Cobain is a stretch, but Nirvana, at that time, gave Cobain a sort of equilibrium: writing, singing, playing guitar, the concerts, the audience. For a moment, they seemed to let him live the life

WITH DAVE GROHL, THE SOUND OF THE BAND TOOK SHAPE

he had always dreamed of. And the fact that everything seemed possible surely played its part too. Around the same time that they found the third fundamental element, they began contacting new record labels through a lawyer (David Mintz). That led to Nirvana signing a contract with the David Geffen Company, the same one that their heroes and mentors Sonic Youth had settled down with. It was destined to be the label that would soon release a musical milestone: *Nevermind*.

So, was Cobain a reserved, melancholy guy, uninterested in success and stardom, who breezed through success indifferently, as if it were none of his business, staying punk to his core even after selling millions of albums, though, perhaps more than anything else, guided by the calculating greed of Courtney Love? Or was he a focused strategist who had planned how to climb every rung along the pop-star-system ladder, with laser-sharp control over every aspect of Nirvana's artistic production, far from being a victim to that vampire wife of his as his fans tend to project?

The trio in its definitive configuration: from left, Dave Grohl, Kurt Cobain and Krist Novoselic.

In truth, he probably was both. His manager Danny Goldberg (author of the biography *Serving the Servant: Remembering Kurt Cobain*, 2019), who began working with the band at that exact moment and stayed with them until the end, becoming a close friend of Cobain's and later representing Hole and Love too, confirmed: "Despite the fact that the side effects of fame would disorient and sometimes torment Kurt, it's clear to me in retrospect that success on his own terms was something he had meticulously planned for years. The arc and the intensity of his career was no accident. It was something he did on purpose."

It's an idea that Goldberg repeats frequently throughout the book, highlighting how Cobain was intrigued and greedy over the idea of expanding his audience, yet also uninterested and skeptical of the hardcore punk fundamentalism that sees every album sold in a shop, every contract with a professional, organized record label as a cog in the wheel of the "capitalist" enemy to destroy. Curious and attentive at the meetings with record label execs (speaking to them politely, as his peers, without provocative stances), Cobain had a clear vision even of the secondary aspects of Nirvana's albums: what images to put on the covers, how to make their music videos, etc.

Nirvana on a sidewalk in Shepherd's Bush, London, 1990.

As Everett True mentions in his band biography, Cobain and Novoselic often would invent crazy stories about their lives as "ignorant lumberjacks" to reinforce the cliches that the music press was weaving around those in the Pacific Northwest scene, with their flannel shirts, ripped jeans and untied combat boots. Cobain had created this raw yet naïve character and narrative, to then rip it apart by proving to be the intellectually sophisticated person that he was, and even complaining about it as "persecution," although he knew he had built the persona himself by spreading exuberant rumors.

The humor with which Cobain looked at all the hysteria and hang-ups in the rock scene has also been confirmed by Craig Montgomery, the sound engineer hired by Sub Pop to tour with the band. "Smashing their gear was part of the game. It was a tribute and a critique at the same time. [Kurt] was fun, intelligent, sharp and sarcastic. Most of the time, it was a pleasure to be around him. Every so often, he got quiet and he needed to be alone, but playing on stage was his life." Deep down, as Goldberg also noted, "Kurt wanted to be accepted by all the different sides of his inner teenager." He identified so closely with young dropout punkers, but he equally embraced the chance to be appreciated by a broader audience "thanks to a catchy refrain or a nice riff." And, as his friends remember, he never missed a chance to mix Black Flag with a few ABBA songs at parties.

in the studio only after the recording of the first eight songs.

But let's go in order: Bruce Pavitt from Sub Pop suggested Butch Vig as the potential producer of the second Nirvana album, known for having shaped the heavy sound of Killdozer, which Nirvana had said they wanted to move towards. So, the group moved from Seattle to Vig's Smart Studios in Wisconsin. In the first round, they recorded eight songs: "Breed" (initially plus the slightly less famous "Come as You Are" (second single), "Territorial Pissings," "Drain You," "Lounge Act," "Stay Away," "On a Plain," and "Something in the Way."

From left: Dave Grohl, Kurt Cobain and Krist Novoselic in London on August 20, 1991, while promoting Nevermind.

ROCK WAS ONCE AGAIN
A WAY TO EXPRESS THE
RAGE AND DREAMS OF
A GENERATION

A Nirvana concert in 1991.

THE BAND WENT TO CALIFORNIA TO RECORD THE ALBUM

The sessions lasted sixteen days, recorded at Sound City Studios in Van Nuys, California: for the first time, the members of Nirvana found themselves recording in the room next to that of one of their idols, Ozzy Osbourne, writing his name on their knuckles, even though they did not even dare to meet him afterwards! In that SoCal studio, the group worked eight to ten hours each day: Novoselic and Grohl would actually finish their respective parts (bass and drums) in a few days, while Cobain had to work harder on his own guitar playing, overdubs, singing and especially the lyrics, which were still being fine-tuned right up until recording. Vig once recounted a curious anecdote about the sessions: to convince a reluctant Cobain to dub his vocal track for "In Bloom," he told him that "even John Lennon dubbed his voice." Only when presented with that justification, Cobain, a huge admirer of the author of "Imagine," folded to the technique of dubbing without so much as batting an eye.

Cobain crowd surfing at a concert in Frankfurt, Germany, November 12, 1991.

Unfortunately, while the sessions were drawing to a close, Vig also recounted that Cobain became increasingly introverted and hard to manage: "He could be in an elated mood, ready to play, then half an hour later he'd just sit in a corner and not say anything to anybody."

Those episodes were probably the first visible warning signs of the malaise that Cobain had carried within him since childhood, the combination of physical pain and psychological distress mentioned earlier, that neither artistic success, nor fame, nor apparent sentimental (or familial) satisfaction—even in a family in which the needles had continued to circulate—had ever managed to soothe. Malaise that "Smells Like Teen Spirit" expressed, becoming an emblem of an entire generation, and even the ones after it. All that, in spite of seemingly rambling, at times incomprehensible lyrics, which perfectly convey the "randomness" employed by Cobain in composing his verses.

Lyrics that upon first inspection are a bit nonsensical, composed of everyday phrases that seem almost haphazardly slapped together. And yet, aside from the play on words about the teen deodorant used by Tobi Vail, the sense of disorientation that defined Generation X, the boredom and fear of that generation (absent in lyrics from the '68 cohort), come through loud and clear. Then add the perennial urge to destroy it all (expressed perfectly in the song's video, supervised by Cobain, who personally designed the story board) with the arrogance that comes with all adolescence ("I feel stupid, and contagious"). And also, the immortal "Here we are now, entertain us," which proclaims a very punk rock right to over-the-top amusement, which however is aimed at a "you" that, despite not being very specific, supposes that someone is in fact listening to that imperative, someone probably less "stupid and contagious," but who is there as the recipient of the demands of the "teen spirit" (in the literal sense). Adults, perhaps? Neither the lyrics nor their author ever really shed light on the matter (to the contrary, he scolded journalists who "came up with second-hand Freudian interpretations" of his lyrics). However, it certainly can be inferred. All this highlights another detail specific to the grunge rebellion of the 1990s: it is predicated upon its existence before the eyes of an "other" ("here we are") from which something is expected, even if that something is merely frivolous ("entertain us"). It's something that perhaps neither the young Stooges nor the Sex Pistols would have ever asked of the adult world, which they instead set out to shock or at most ignore, as if it were completely non-existent.

A portrait of Kurt Cobain taken on August 31, 1991, in Rotterdam, Netherlands.

A picture of Nirvana (from left: Dave Grohl, Krist
Novoselic and Kurt Cobain) taken in Rotterdam,
Netherlands, on August 31, 1991.

Another portrait of the band taken by
Niels van Iperen on August 31, 1991, in
Rotterdam, Netherlands. From left: Dave
Grohl, Kurt Cobain and Krist Novoselic.

Nevermind was released on September 24, 1991: Geffen Records expected it to perform like any good alternative rock album, meaning a maximum of 250,000 copies sold, a bit like *Goo*, the DGC debut album of Nirvana mentors Sonic Youth. This determined how the album was distributed: 46,000 copies to stores in the U.S., and a solid 35,000 to those in England, where *Bleach* had been received quite positively. And that's how the album's path to success began, like any great alternative rock album fully promoted by a major label on college radio and FM stations specialized in the sub-genre. From there, however, the "Smells Like Teen Spirit" single (which had come out on September 10) went into frequent rotation even on the radio stations dedicated to heavy metal, then even on those geared towards the rock/pop mainstream. Nirvana had performed a miracle by uniting different audiences that, up until that moment, were irreconcilable. Even the video ended up in heavy rotation on MTV, eventually becoming the most played by the channel. As such, the album, which had debuted in 144th place on the Billboard 200, reached the Billboard Top 40 for the first time, climbing up to number 35 when the band was about to leave for a promotional tour in Europe. And it didn't stop there: on January 11, 1992, it became Nirvana's first number one album, dethroning, as we mentioned, Michael Jackson's colossal *Dangerous*. By then, *Nevermind* was selling 300,000 copies—the amount the label had expected to sell overall—per week. As always happens in these cases, even the cover of the album became an iconic symbol of the era, the style, the ironic attitude of the group in relation to the success that was engulfing it, and grunge in general. That photograph was another one of Cobain's inventions, after having seen the pictures of a news report on water births. The image was completed in post-production, adding the dollar hanging on a fishing hook to a shot recreated by photographer Kirk Weddle, who snapped a four-month-old in a swimming pool at the Aquatics Center in Pasadena, California.

On this occasion, Cobain fiercely opposed the idea of creating an alternative version of the cover that didn't show the baby's penis, to avoid possible indecency claims, saying "anyone who would be offended by the image of a newborn's penis was probably a closeted pedophile."

The baby's parents were paid somewhere between $150 and $200 for the use of their "little star," even if then the band gave them the gold album award it earned as a sign of recognition after its widespread success. But that wasn't enough. At the age of 15 (in 2005), Spencer Elden, the baby in the picture, was in a documentary about the album (and later in other interviews, such as that with *NME*) in which he said he was delighted to have been part of rock history, recreating the scene (in board shorts) in the same pool as in 2008, even getting *Nevermind* tattooed on his chest. But in the end, he decided to sue them all: Grohl, Novoselic, Cobain's estate, the record label and the photographer, asking for $150,000 in damages for having been "exploited" without his consent (his father, Nick, testified that the photographer asked to take a few pictures of the boy without having stated his intentions), due to the picture's presumed and absurd uncensored "child pornography," and because it caused him "permanent harm" later in life. On September 2, 2022, the case was dismissed without cause to prosecute, but in 2023 a US appeals court revived the lawsuit. "This procedural setback does not change our view. We will defend this meritless case with vigor and expect to prevail," stated a lawyer for the defendants. But without a doubt, the cover with the "money-hungry" baby is still there, containing the most famous grunge album there ever was.

The cover of Nevermind, *released September 24, 1991.*

The second single from *Nevermind* was "Come as You Are." According to record execs, it was the track, the one that was supposed to be a crossover between the alternative/punk and mainstream audiences, for its greater melodic appeal. Despite the trench that divides alternative and mainstream audiences having already been brilliantly crossed by "Smells Like Teen Spirit," "Come as You Are" served to reinforce the disruptive power of the album that got the whole world head banging. It was the group's number two single in terms of sales, and the 2019 year-end report published by Nielsen Music certified it as the third-most-played song of the decade on mainstream rock stations, with 134,000 spins. In the album's press kit, Cobain stated that "Come as You Are" was "an old-fashioned love song coming down in three-part harmony." One verse stands out in particular: "I swear that I don't have a gun," which many have taken to be a tragic prophecy of the still-distant end of the singer, even if the temporal distance from his suicide suggests more of a coincidence between a metaphor that could be interpreted as "I swear I don't have anything to hide" and the unhealthy attraction Cobain had for guns, which would come out later on. Gold in France and Germany, "Come as You Are" went platinum in Italy, double-platinum in Great Britain and 4x platinum in Australia. And, if you go on a pilgrimage to Aberdeen, Cobain's hometown, "Come as You Are" has even become the welcome phrase that greets you from the signpost at the

"COME AS YOU ARE" BECAME THE SLOGAN ON ROAD SIGNS WELCOMING VISITORS TO THE TOWN OF ABERDEEN, WASHINGTON

city's limits. "Lithium" was chosen as the third single for the record-breaking album, released on July 13, 1992: musically, it's a perfect example of the style that came out of the *Nevermind* sessions, alternating quiet, melodic moments with abrupt breaks and thunderous transitions. Cobain once said that the song was about a man who found comfort in religion after his girlfriend died, as a "final lifeline before suicide." And, although the narrator is fictional, it's hard not to see slivers of the singer's personality in the lyrics, a narrator whose "friends are in his head," who is "so lonely...I shaved my head." The finding God lyric could be a reference to the temporary period in which young Kurt lived at the home of his friend Jesse Reed, whose parents were ardent born-again Christians. But then again, real-world lithium is no balm for religious rituals, quite the contrary.

It's a powerful calming psychiatric medication used to treat bipolar disorder and major depressive disorder, which perhaps the singer hadn't yet fallen prey to at the time, though he probably did feel their rumblings deep within.

Nevermind then gave rise to a fourth single, placing "In Bloom" on the podium. It was one of the first tracks created by the trio for the new album in 1990, recorded with Vig, still thinking of Sub Pop as the label. A rather noisy and powerful grunge track, "In Bloom" reached number five on the U.S. charts, and was certified silver in Great Britain and platinum in Australia, where Nirvana hit it big with practically every release.

However, once they had finished recording, the band and producer were dissatisfied with the mixing of the tracks, so they resolved to find someone external to the team to put on the mixing board's faders: setting aside Scott Litt (known for his work with R.E.M.) and Ed Stasium (who had already worked with the Smithereens and who had been proposed by Geffen but Cobain feared would give the album a sound too similar to that of other groups), Andy Wallace was chosen, already at the helm of "Season in the Abyss" by the killer thrash metal group Slayer. Yet, even his mixing was initially viewed as "too clean" by the group: Cobain was "embarrassed" by his second album sounding "closer to a Mötley Crüe record than it is a punk rock record." Only with time, like a fine wine, both Nirvana and Vig agreed that the final result of the in-studio production work was fully satisfactory.

Kurt Cobain during a recording session at Wisseloord Studio, in Hilversum, Netherlands, on November 25, 1991. Following pages: The entire group during the same recording session.

1991

Above and opposite: Kurt Cobain during the recording session at Wisseloord Studio in Hilversum, Netherlands.

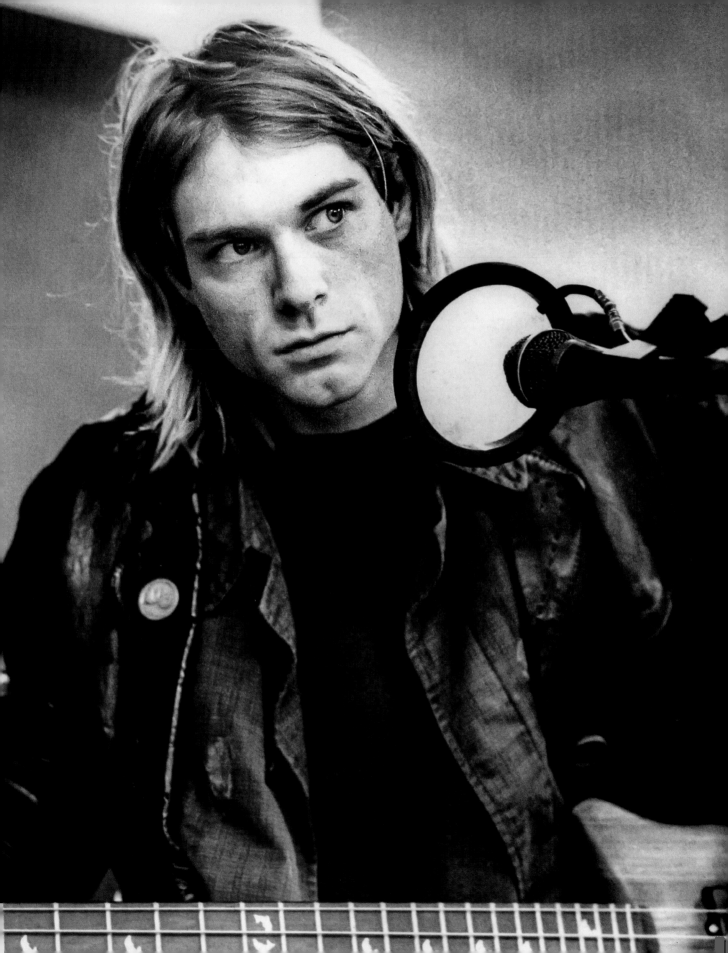

At left and above: Two more pictures of Cobain during the session at Wisseloord Studio in Hilversum, Netherlands, on November 25, 1991.

Nirvana in 1991 (from left: Dave Grohl, Kurt Cobain, and Krist Novoselic).

"You only appreciate things when they're gone."

A curious image of Nirvana taken in a bathroom. From left: Krist Novoselic, Dave Grohl and, lower down, Kurt Cobain.

Above: A portrait of Cobain, taken in Rotterdam on August 31, 1991.

Opposite: Nirvana photographed on the same day (Krist Novoselic is on the left,
Kurt Cobain in the center, Dave Grohl to the right).

1991

Above: Krist Novoselic (left) and Kurt Cobain (right) on stage at the Paradiso, Amsterdam, on November 25, 1991.

Opposite and pages 106-107: Cobain during the same concert.

"Punk rock
is art.
Punk rock
is freedom."

| KURT COBAIN

Previous page: Cobain on stage at the Reading Festival, England, on August 23, 1991.

Opposite: Cobain on stage with Eugene Kelly of the Vaselines.

Above: Cobain again, during the same performance at Reading.

NEVERMIND RADICALLY CHANGED THE FACE OF ROCK

Cobain on stage at the Reading Festival on August 23, 1991.

Opposite and above: Cobain on stage as he performs with Nirvana at the Pukkelpop Festival in Hasselt, Belgium, on August 25, 1991.

Following two pages: Nirvana on stage, guests of a television show.

Pages 118 and 119: Two images of Cobain at the Reading Festival on August 23, 1991.

Above and opposite: The frontman of Nirvana on stage at the London Astoria,
May 11, 1991.

1991

Opposite and above: Kurt Cobain during the Nirvana concert at the Forum in Los Angeles, December 27, 1991.

The year 1991 was also the year in which Kurt Cobain and Courtney Love's relationship was made public. They had met in 1989 and Cobain had been impressed by her look and her punk attitude. They had seen each other a few times starting in 1990, and each time, Cobain admired her platinum blond hair, her brazenness and her excessive vitality. They fought from day one, but they were also intensely attracted to each another. It was love, without a doubt, but also aggression, tension and instability, but the couple, incredibly, worked. Legend has it that, after a fight, Love sent Cobain (using Grohl as a messenger) a perfumed heart-shaped box with a porcelain doll, three dried roses, a miniature teacup and shells to ask for forgiveness. It was the "Heart-Shaped Box" that Cobain turned into music for his famous song. Love hadn't had an easy childhood, with rather particular parents: a hippie psychotherapist mother and a father

who was road manager to the Grateful Dead (in the divorce filings between them, Love's mother had even accused him of giving little Courtney LSD). Her teen years weren't any easier, with an arrest for theft at fourteen years old. Music and performing were in her blood, in any case, and in 1981 she was already in Liverpool hanging out with the entourage of the Teardrop Explodes and Echo and the Bunnymen. In 1984, she got her first band together, and in 1988, Hole was born.

Kurt and Courtney got married on February 24, 1992, on a beach in Waikiki, Hawaii. She wore a white dress, he donned pajamas and a patchwork crossbody bag, and both held a bouquet of flowers. In the pictures of that day, they're smiling, happy and radiant. In August of that same year, their daughter, Frances Bean, was born. As everyone knows by now, Courtney Love was more than a wife to Kurt Cobain; she was, in no small measure, also his muse. However, it's equally true that Nirvana had hit it big before they met, so it should have been Cobain, despite being three years younger than Love, to be the point of reference to the spouse that yearned for pop glory. However, in the relationship, Love was the more concrete one, apparently able to manage success and its consequences, to calculate costs and benefits, to see things in perspective, while Cobain remained the moody adolescent who suffered and dreamed.

In turn, a legend cropped up around this aspect of their relationship, propelled by the fact that the two even called each other "John" and "Yoko," in reference to the relationship between Lennon and Ono, who was equally hated by Beatles fans around the world as an "opportunist" and presumed cause of the breakup of the Fab Four. Just after having signed the contract to manage Nirvana, Danny Goldberg, who surely knew Love better than many of her detractors as he was the manager of Hole too, said: "Courtney was 27 at the time, three years older than Kurt, and a force to be reckoned with...she made a beeline for the back of the dressing room, where Kurt was sitting. Although she was several inches taller than he was, Courtney was soon perched on Kurt's lap. They each had grins on their faces like the proverbial cat that swallowed the canary. It was the first night that Kurt and Courtney slept together. By the time of Rock for Choice benefit two weeks later, Kurt and Courtney were a couple, and it would stay that way for the rest of Kurt's life. Courtney took and gave offense very easily, but I loved her sense of humor and her intelligence. Although others around Nirvana seemed to think that the liaison would last no longer than a typically evanescent rock-and-roll fling, it was soon obvious to me that Kurt was deeply in love with Courtney and that the feeling was mutual." One can deduce that the love between them was truly similar to that of John Lennon and Yoko Ono, aside from the joking of the two involved parties, and they probably influenced each other, though it is probably also misleading to think of Love as a "cruel sorceress Circe" and manipulator of an ill-equipped eternally adolescent rocker. "Kurt had unique talent and he was much more successful. Courtney had more street smarts and a broader awareness of culture," continued Goldberg. "She was a remarkable lyricist and compelling performer with a media sophistication that rivaled Kurt's."

Goldberg also mentioned a statement by Love herself: "I was sure I would bring even Madonna down, and Kurt liked that part of my personality. He was ambitious but he hid it really well." Too ambitious, it is said, to get along for an extended period of time with the riot grrls in Olympia that she had taken her first steps with. And although she became a star, her discography is relatively scant: just four albums with Hole from 1991 to 2010, plus a solo album in 2004 and not much more than a handful of random singles and a few collaborations over the years. In short, not much for a career that essentially seemed to focus more on the glamour of Oscar Night than the rock stage.

Opposite: Courtney Love, the leader of Hole, and Kurt Cobain of Nirvana, backstage in 1991.
Following pages: Courtney Love and Kurt Cobain in New York on January 10, 1992.

Above and opposite: Kurt Cobain during the press conference held by the band in Japan at the Roppongi Prince Hotel in Tokyo on February 18, 1992.

In any case, the success of *Nevermind* rapidly transformed grunge into the "new punk of the entire world" and soon it all (songs, band, sound, Seattle scene, even the characteristic sloppy clothing) became the new trend for the 1990s. Soon even "real" fashion magazines hurried to embrace the new Northwest lumberjack look. Grunge became trendy, which actually wasn't so surprising. After all, all subcultures that arise as a challenge to some sort of idea of the "middle class," "conservatism," or simply "normality," and then gain a certain following, become fashionable. It happened with the mods, with the miniskirts of Mary Quant and bob haircuts, and hippies, with their long untamed locks and bell bottoms, and even the fetish-punk of Vivienne Westwood. Heavy metal brought biker-style cool to the mainstream with leather jackets and bandanas, hip hop turned athleisure into a racial signifier and so on, in an incessant movement from the edges to the core of the global market. Grunge musicians simply performed on stage in the clothes they wore every day in the cloudy climate of the Pacific Northwest, with "patent lumberjack shirts and ugly '50s geometric-patterned sweaters" (as defined by music journalist Christopher Sandford). "People were wearing flannel here long before grunge came out. It's cold here. It's a cheap and effective clothing apparatus for living in the Northwest," rightly highlighted Tad Doyle of Tad. "I wore shorts year-round. I rode bikes everywhere, didn't

New music generates new trends, and young people soon adopted "grunge" fashion: plaid flannel shirts and baggy jeans

have a car, and if I was going to practice, I had to carry my bass on my bicycle, so I couldn't wear jeans," echoed Jeff Ament of Pearl Jam. "I'm not sure what defined what grunge was or wasn't. I never ever wore a flannel shirt. I had a few hats, for sure. That started off when I was in Green River and had a girlfriend who made hats. At the time, I don't think I looked like a rocker, I looked like a dumbass. It was partly function

Kurt Cobain on stage at the MTV Video Music Awards on September 10, 1992.

and partly what was laying around," he continued. However, when tour manager Eric Johnson stated, "I met the Soundgarden guys when I booked them for a show in Ellensburg, in '86 or '87...They all had work pants on and boots rolled up, and Chris looked like he just got done workin' in a steel yard. I thought they looked so cool," it was clear that their particular kind of "casual" had made an impression. It had become a new style. Sure, it would take the mainstream success of *Nevermind* for glossy magazines around the globe to start publishing editorials with models bundled up in checkered shirts, raw wool sweaters and wool beanies, but soon enough grunge became synonymous even with a sort of shabby and (seemingly) anti-fashion look. In 2014, Vogue wrote that "Cobain pulled liberally from both ends of a woman's and a man's wardrobe, and his Seattle thrift-store look ran the gamut of masculine lumberjack workwear and 40s-by-way-of-70s feminine dresses. It was completely counter to the shellacked, flashy aesthetic of the 1980s in every way. In disheveled jeans and floral frocks, he softened the tough exterior of the archetypal rebel from the inside out, and set the ball in motion for a radical, millennial ideal of androgyny." Kurt's personal style was, in short, "the antithesis of the macho American man. At a time when a body-conscious silhouette was the defining look, he made it cooler to look slouchy and loose, no matter if you were a boy or a girl."

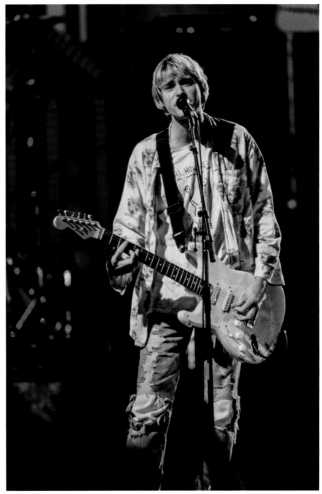

Writer Julianne Escobedo Shepherd confirmed Cobain's style of dress with greater depth: "He didn't just make it OK to be a freak, he made it desirable." Even if, according to music journalist Charles R. Cross, the Nirvana frontman "was just too lazy to shampoo." Basically, the less he spent on clothing, the more he earned in style. Jonathan Poneman of Sub Pop said: "This [clothing] is cheap, it's durable, and it's kind of timeless. It also runs against the grain of the whole flashy esthetic that existed in the '80s. Grunge fashion was very much an anti-fashion response and a non-conformist move against the 'manufactured image' of bands."

But let's get back to the music. We've already highlighted the gap that had always separated Cobain from the hair metal bands of the 1980s, in spite of the fact that the success of Nirvana had in part bridged the gap between their respective audiences (or at least between the open-minded camps on each side).

But the biggest rift was the one between Kurt Cobain and Axl Rose of Guns N' Roses. It's important to remember that Axl Rose, well-seasoned in the field of media scuffles, scandals, and taking stances that were far from politically correct well before *Nevermind* came out, had publicly praised Nirvana, even flaunting one of their beanies while filming the "Don't Cry" music video. But that praise wasn't returned by "progressive" Cobain, who probably feared being confused with that troublesome congregation of sexist, chauvinist, homophobic (and worse) rockers. "We're not your typical Guns N' Roses type of band that has absolutely nothing to say," Cobain told *Seconds* at the time. And the following year, he repeated the concept during an interview with a publication from Singapore, stating, "Rebellion is standing up to people like Guns N' Roses." Goldberg has noted that, on October 27, 1991, about one month after *Nevermind* was released, Nirvana played at the Palace Theatre in Los Angeles, the hometown of Geffen: on that occasion, a record executive told Nirvana's manager that he was heading backstage to say hello to the band and that Axl Rose was coming with him. Cobain categorically refused to meet his unwelcome peer, so Goldberg had to come up with a wise diplomatic refusal so as not to inflame any egos, giving the backstage passes to Rose but sneaking out from the back of the theater with Kurt at just the right moment. That way, Rose

IN 1992, A FEUD BEGAN BETWEEN KURT COBAIN AND AXL ROSE OF GUNS N' ROSES

"randomly" found the dressing room empty, as often happens in the chaos of a rock concert, thereby avoiding the risk of running into Rose during their getaway. The strategy worked, but it was clear that Rose didn't appreciate their absence. A documented report in *Rolling Stone* (April 11, 2016) states that in 1992 Rose was determined to bring Nirvana on tour as his band's opening act. "Guns N' Roses was about to do this massive stadium tour with Metallica, and they wanted us to open," Grohl later recalled.

30, Axl had been calling Kurt nonstop. One day we're walking through an airport and Kurt says, 'F**k. Axl Rose won't stop calling me.'" But even the patience of a Guns N' Roses fan has a limit, and the fuse is much shorter for someone like Rose: in the end, during one of those Nirvana-less concerts, Rose harangued the audience on the concept of "alternative rockers": "the only thing that means to me is someone like Kurt Cobain and Nirvana, who is basically just a f**kin' junkie with a junkie wife. And if the baby's born deformed, I think they both oughta go to prison."

The bandana-wearing blond, with his usual sensitivity, which had become proverbial even in the colorful chronicles of rock, referred to the rumors that Frances Bean, Kurt and Courtney's daughter, could be born with a disability due to her parents' drug use. As *Rolling Stone* once again outlined, the feud reached its boiling point during the MTV Video Music Awards in 1992. While backstage, Rose and his long-time girlfriend, model Stephanie Seymour, walked past Kurt and Courtney, who were sitting with their daughter. Love began taunting Rose, asking him to be the godfather of their child, and Rose responded, directing his rage at Cobain: "You shut your bitch up, or I'm taking you down to the pavement!" In disbelief, Cobain turned to Love, and sarcastically said, "Shut up, bitch!" Just like a true metal macho. The authors of the article, Keith Harris and Kory Grow, note that the tension extended even to the bassists of the bands, Duff McKagan and Krist Novoselic, who also exchanged a few harsh words backstage. Years later, in an interview, Cobain confessed to having spit on Rose's keyboard while on stage: "I spit on Axl's keyboards, it was either that or

beat him up...I saw his piano there and I thought, oh, I have to take this opportunity, and I spit big goobers all over his keyboards. I hope he didn't get it off in time." Later on, he would remember that tiff while backstage at the MTV Video Music Awards, once again insulting Guns N' Roses, as musicians and as people: "Axl Rose is a f**king sexist and a racist and a homophobe, and you can't be on his side and be on our side. I'm sorry that I have to divide this up like this, but it's something you can't ignore. And besides, Guns N' Roses can't write good music." Just before Cobain's death, the waters seemed to have calmed a bit: the singer flew to Seattle seated next to the G N' R bassist Duff McKagan, amicably talking about mutual friends and drug rehab (a common denominator for both "families"), even if, once off the plane, Cobain had already vanished while the bass player was thinking of offering him a ride home. Grohl has said that, when Cobain died, the first condolences he received on his voice mail were from Matt Sorum, the former member of the Cult who had become the permanent bassist of Guns N' Roses: "Man, I'm really sorry, and I hope you're doing well." McKagan eventually owned up to his rash behavior at the 1992 VMAs: "I blew my lid when I perceived a slander toward my band from the Nirvana camp. In my drunken haze and drug-induced mania, I heard what I wanted to hear, and I went after Krist Novoselic backstage. I had no control of myself then. And Krist, I am sorry for that day." Having re-established a "milk and honey" understanding between the two hard rock camps, time (the soother of so many hostilities) would even provide a shot at musical collaboration between members of G N' R and the remaining members of Nirvana.

"It's fun to fight. It gives you something to do. It relieves boredom."

| KURT COBAIN

A picture of Nirvana in 1992 (from above: Krist Novoselic, Dave Grohl and Kurt Cobain).

1992

A nice picture of Cobain during a private moment
backstage in Belfast, 1992.

SUCCESS MADE COBAIN'S LIFE MORE INTENSE, BUT ALSO MORE DIFFICULT

Above and opposite: Kurt Cobain enjoying a quiet moment in his room at the Roppongi Prince Hotel in Tokyo on December 19, 1992.

5

1993–1994
THE SUCCESS,
THE STRUGGLE,
THE END

FROM THE TOP
OF THE WORLD TO THE
DEEPEST ABYSS

We ended the previous chapter in 1992, with the worldwide success of *Nevermind*. But, beyond the album that would take Nirvana from underground to stardom, from indie grunge to mainstream, that year was also full of important events in the personal and familial life of Cobain. So much so that it would be a watershed year, with a before and an after. Let's take a look at those events in rapid succession: On February 24, Cobain and Love got married in Waikiki, Hawaii. The ceremony was very low-key, almost hurried and without superstar guests, and something that not even the bride and groom talked

On February 24, 1992, Kurt Cobain and Courtney Love got married in Waikiki, Hawaii

about very much. But in the meantime, rumors were spreading about the growing heroin use of both punk spouses. On August 12, *Vanity Fair* published a long article on Love (which she herself requested) by Lynn Hirschberg. The result was a heavy-handed portrait of the Hole frontwoman, and thus also of the indie-rock couple in general, categorizing them as a drug-addicted pair of degenerates à la Sid and Nancy, a danger to their unborn daughter who was already in the media crosshairs. The article stated that Love still was using heroin even though she was pregnant, something that she only admitted to many years later. Six days after the article came out, on August 18, Frances Bean Cobain was born: the daughter of the two musicians was perfectly healthy in spite of all the rumors and today is a visual artist and model.

However, the *Vanity Fair* article weighed heavy as a boulder on the image of both parents, to the point that even Cedars-Sinai Medical Center in Los Angeles, where Love gave birth, went so far as to falsify health records and disclose confidential information to the media about the child's mother. This pushed social services to take Frances Bean away from them, placing her in temporary custody of Love's half-sister, Jaime Manelli, who in the state's eyes was the most stable person in a family that, unfortunately, was troubled on both sides.

That article, as Cobain later told Jon Savage, launched a terrible press campaign: "That started it. There were probably 50 more articles based on that story. I'd never paid attention to the mainstream press or media before, so I wasn't aware of people being attacked and crucified on that level. I can't help but feel that we've been scapegoated, in a way. I have a lot of animosity towards journalists and the press in general. Because it's happening to me, of course, I'm probably exaggerating it, but I can't think of another example of a current band that's had more negative articles written about them... A lot of it is just simple sexism. Courtney is my wife, and a lot of people could not accept the fact that I'm in love, and that I could be happy. Because she's such a powerful person, and such a threatening person, every sexist within the industry just joined forces and decided to string us up."

Things got really, truly bad. Journalists were searching for any possible story to create a scandal around Kurt and Courtney, who everyone saw as the Sid Vicious and Nancy Spungen of the 1990s. Their story was a perfect tale of love, drugs, excess, perdition, success, beauty, fame and desperation, the kind that could fill pages and pages of magazines. The attention paid to the two was enormous, constant and overblown.

Page 143: The Cobain family: Kurt and his wife, Courtney, who holds their daughter, little Frances Bean, in her arms.

Opposite and above: A happy Kurt Cobain, with his daughter Frances Bean.

Despite someone in the Nirvana entourage comparing Cobain to a dying ruin, on August 30, Nirvana played one of the most memorable concerts of their short yet dazzling career at Reading Festival in England. Cobain took to the stage in a wheelchair, wearing a white hospital gown, pushed along by his journalist-biographer-friend Everett True, a sarcastic commentary on the rumors that said he was essentially terminally ill, singing the opening of "The Rose" by Bette Midler (from the film of the same name, in which Midler plays a star who dies of an overdose, loosely based on Janis Joplin). He then fell to the ground, only to jump back up like the James Brown of grunge, screeching out with all his might "Breed," one of the most hysterically punk tracks on *Nevermind*. Those in the audience, all 80,000 of them, were right there with him. Nirvana was once again riding the wave, despite the rumors.

On September 9, although reluctantly, Cobain agreed to play at the MTV Video Music Awards. He even swallowed the broadcaster's rejection of "Rape Me" (like "Tourette's," played at Reading with the provisory title "The Eagle Has Landed"), one of the new tracks that would later end up on *In Utero*, then feared to be understood as a promotion of rape,

On August 30, 1993, Cobain put on a real show, taking to the stage in a wheelchair, an ironic commentary on his health.

in spite of the clear feminist stance of the songwriter. Nirvana fell back on the well-established "Lithium" and Cobain even was congratulated by Peter Gabriel, and he even got to meet his teenage idols Queen, as a superstar. Unfortunately, that concert was also the backdrop to the fight with Axl Rose.

Kurt Cobain wearing a blond wig on stage at the Reading Festival on August 30, 1993.

Above and opposite: Two shots from the historic Nirvana concert at the Reading Festival on August 30, 1993.

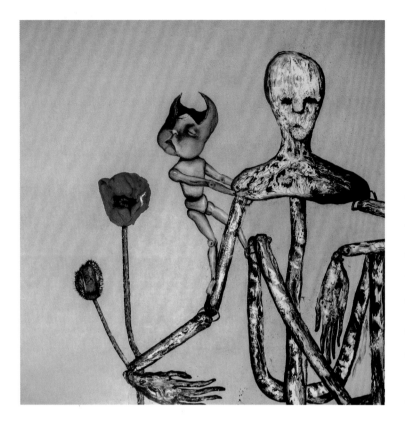

Above: The front cover of
Incesticide.
Opposite: The back cover of the
same album.

Around that time, Cobain met director Gus
Van Sant, who would be the one to immortalize
the last tragic days of the singer's life in the
appropriately titled *The Last Days*. And, a few
days before Christmas, the year closed out with
the release of *Incesticide*, which was originally
supposed to be called "Throwaways" (or, not-so-
subtly, "Cash Cow"). However, to many it sounded
like a new Nirvana album, dry and brutal like in
the good old days. Indeed, *Incesticide* essentially
was an album from the early days: devastating
tracks such as "Aero Zeppelin," "Hairspray Queen" and "Mexican Seafood" were
even plucked from 1988. They included some tracks already out on lesser
releases, covers of other artists, unreleased songs and B-sides from singles,
plus three new ones. The covers were "Molly's Lips" and "Son of a Gun" by the
Vaselines, one of Kurt's favorite bands, plus Devo's "Turnaround" from the
Hormoaning EP, released only in Australia and Japan. The other tracks were
B-sides from singles or alternative versions of previously released songs,
including the standout "(New Wave) Polly," which was a harder, more frenetic
version of "Polly," already famous for the more melodic version on *Nevermind*.
Kurt was horrified at the news that a true rapist had sung his song to a
victim, spurring him to become even more explicit in his anti-sexist stance,
resulting in "Rape Me" on *In Utero*. Given the varied sources of the material on
Incesticide, all of the drummers that had cycled through Nirvana over time
were on the compilation. The cover art, on the other hand, was once again

1 DIVE
2 SLIVER
3 STAIN
4 BEEN A SON
5 TURNAROUND
6 MOLLY'S LIPS
7 SON OF A GUN
8 (NEW WAVE) POLLY
9 BEESWAX
10 DOWNER
11 MEXICAN SEAFOOD
12 HAIRSPRAY QUEEN
13 AERO ZEPPELIN
14 BIG LONG NOW
15 ANEURYSM

all Kurt (actually Kurdt, as he was credited in the liner notes), even more so than on *Bleach* and *Nevermind*, because here, for the first time, the cover was a drawing by Cobain's own hand. Like the album it illustrated, it also was titled "Incesticide," and it marked the start of a stream of "uterine" references to procreation and femininity that, though already being present among the singer's sensitivity to the other half of the sky, were even more prominent in the song titles in the second part of the group's career. On the back was a close-up of a fun rubber ducky, which Cobain seemed to have amassed a collection of even before becoming a father. On the inside, a picture of the band in perfect, chaotic Sub Pop-style, but in color, accompanied by an explosive statement by the singer, no stranger to programmatic proclamations to affirm the essence of his art, to justify his choices, to refute criticism or gossip, to reiterate a punk spirit or to criticize its fundamentalism: "I don't feel the least bit guilty for commercially exploiting a completely exhausted Rock youth Culture because, at this point in rock history, Punk Rock (while still sacred to some) is, to me, dead and gone. We just wanted to pay tribute to something that helped us to feel as though we

had crawled out of the dung heap of conformity.

To pay tribute like an Elvis or Jimi Hendrix impersonator in the tradition of a bar band. I'll be the first to admit that we're the '90s version of Cheap Trick or the Knack but the last to admit that it hasn't been rewarding." Although it was minimally publicized by Geffen in order not to inflate the market of Nirvana products ahead of the release of the band's third studio album, scheduled for the following year, *Incesticide* sold about 500,000 copies within two months of its release, certified gold in France and platinum in the U.S., Great Britain and Canada. And it gave fans back the Nirvana that they feared might have been watered down by the success of *Nevermind*. A fear that the upcoming *In Utero* would forcefully dispel.

Immediately after the release of *Incesticide*, the group began 1993 with a tour in Brazil, to then take a month-long break. During that month, in February, Cobain granted an interview to *The Advocate*, taking a clear stance in favor of gay rights, something that, it should be noted, was a rarity among entertainment industry stars of the day. In the interview, he confirmed he wasn't gay, but that he was "spiritually," and that if he hadn't met Courtney, he probably would have been bisexual. Just after the interview came out, the band headed to a studio in Cannon Falls, Minnesota, to start working on the third album, the one that, for industry insiders, was to either prove or negate his talent as a songwriter and performer, and the band's staying power at the top of the world. All this, combined with the obsessive media attention, led to tension in Cobain's life, even if the music, as always, seemed to soften the blows, and drugs, in other ways, were a way to escape reality.

In 1993, after a tour in Brazil, the band began working on their third album at a studio in Cannon Falls, Minnesota.

Cobain wanted the new album to be less "clean" than the last one, with a sound that was harder and rawer. So, they called in Steve Albini as the producer. Albini had an impressive resume, as the singer/guitarist of hardcore punk band Big Black and then as the producer behind the sound of the Pixies' *Surfer Rosa* (which surely was an example of punk-pop fusion followed by Cobain), but also of the Jesus Lizard, Pussy Galore, Boss Hog and the Jon Spencer Blues Explosion, in addition to PJ Harvey's *Rid of Me*, all in 1993. He was a one-man trademark when it came to edgy, stinging audio styles, known for routinely crushing vocals below the level of distorted guitars in his mixes.

And this was exactly what happened for *In Utero* as well, the title of which was inspired by a poem written by Courtney Love while pregnant with Frances Bean, chosen over the threatening "I Hate Myself and I Want to Die" that the prophetic singer had initially proposed. The band recorded the 13 tracks from the definitive listing at Pachyderm Recording Studios in Cannon Falls, near Minneapolis, in two weeks of work, but only about six days of proper recording time. Albini had set up about 30 or so mics attached with tape to every corner of the studio, from the floor to the walls, to capture the sound of a live band that Kurt wanted.

"It was a response to the success and sound of *Nevermind*. We just pushed ourselves in the other direction, like, 'Oh really, that's what you like? Well, here's what we're going to f**king do now!'...[it] just came out, like a purge, and it was so pure," Grohl stated in 2021. Steve Albini mixed the album in record time, just five days, working on two or three tracks at a time. The band and Albini were satisfied with the results, but the record label began to pressure the band, not entirely convinced of the overall sound. And perhaps, deep down, Cobain wasn't so sure about it either.

The cover of In Utero, released on September 21, 1993.

THE PRESSURE ON THE BAND AND ON COBAIN, RIDING THE WAVE OF SUCCESS AND SCANDAL, WAS ENORMOUS

A picture of the entire band: Krist Novoselic (above), Kurt Cobain (center), Dave Grohl (below).

Biographer Michael Azerrad (in his book *Come as You Are*, which happened to come out just one week after the album), ironically stated that Cobain loved the idea of a lo-fi philosophy in audio production more than its actual results. Then, Albini himself (perhaps to demonstrate his distance from the relationship with the major record labels) generated new blowback in the media surrounding the band, saying in an interview that "the record label isn't happy with the last Nirvana album," that David Geffen and his management team even hated the result, deeming it "unfit for release," while no representative of the label had even been present at the studio sessions, upon the specific request of the band, which therefore had the blind faith of DGC. In any case, they needed someone to re-mix the album, and again the name of Scott Litt came up (he had been proposed before, for *Nevermind*).

To direct the video of "Heart-Shaped Box," they got Dutch director and photographer Anton Corbijn. It was the last Nirvana music video ever made

Litt got to work right away, finding a perfect groove with the band and with Cobain, whom (despite knowing about his drug use) he found to be "very alert, a perfectionist" and well aware of what he wanted. He added a vocal harmony in "All Apologies" (and the cello, like on "Something in the Way" on the previous album), and in no time at all, the second single was all packed up and ready to go. The first, "Heart-Shaped Box," was finished even faster. For its music video, the director of "Come as You Are" was called again, Kevin Kerslake. But he dared to ask for a budget of almost $500,000, so he was passed over for the talented Dutch photographer Anton Corbijn, who ended up directing "Heart-Shaped Box," the last music video made by Nirvana. He did it by making an exception to his usual way of working, which was to write the video's storyboard on his own. This time, he followed Cobain's instructions, which were "incredibly precise.

More precise than I've ever had for a video. I loved it, but initially I was a bit taken aback...but then looked at it [the idea] and I thought that actually it was pretty good.

I was very amazed by somebody writing a song and having those ideas as precise as he did," explained Corbijn. The video was, for a few weeks, the most played on MTV, winning two awards in 1994: Best Alternative Video and Best Art Direction.

"Junkyard" means garbage dump, but here we'll use it in a more creative, metaphorical sense of "junkie courtyard" to talk about the collaboration between Cobain (Pixie Meat was the nickname given to him by Courtney) and the Beat Generation writer William S. Burroughs (known as "the priest" by his friends for his habitual, severe look of a full suit, complete with a jacket, tie and Borsalino hat). Their meeting was written in the skies, or perhaps in the needles, as detractors might say, seeing as both artists were fans of drugs. Burroughs was a legend to Cobain, not just for his visionary, experimental writing, which inspired generations of rockers before him, but also for his perseverance in his drug use, which didn't stop him from reaching 83 years of age.

In 1992, Cobain wrote Burroughs a respectful, devout letter: he wanted him to appear in the music video for "Heart Shaped-Box," where he envisioned an old man on a cross, and that old man he envisioned as Burroughs himself. The writer declined the offer but sent Cobain a tape containing a recording of him reading "The Junky's Christmas." Cobain went to the recording studio, scrambled the notes of "Silent Night" on his guitar and then those of "To Anacreon in Heaven" (the eighteenth-century composition upon which "The Star-Spangled Banner" was based). In 1993, the independent label Tim/Kerr released a 10" single recorded on just one side (on the back, the signatures of the co-creators) with the reading accompanied by Cobain's experimental guitar playing in "Metal Machine Music" style, titled *The "Priest" They Called Him*. On the cover was a picture taken by the director Gus Van Sant, portraying Krist Novoselic dressed as the priest in the title.

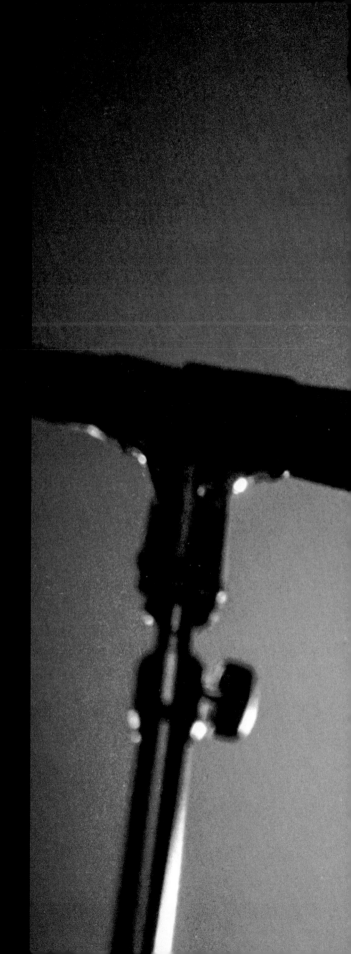

After the creation of this rather unusual disc, the
two met, just once, in October 1993, at Burroughs's
house in Kansas. Burroughs was 79 years old and he
was very fragile physically, but evidently still lucid
and empathetic: "Kurt was very shy, very polite, and
obviously enjoyed the fact that I wasn't awestruck at
meeting him. There was something about him, fragile
and engagingly lost. He smoked cigarettes but didn't
drink. There were no drugs; the topic didn't even
come up," Burroughs stated in an interview following
Cobain's death, which took place six months after their
meeting. "The thing I remember about him is the deathly
grey complexion of his cheeks. It wasn't an act of will
for Kurt to kill himself. As far as I was concerned, he
was dead already."

*At right and following pages: Kurt Cobain while playing at the
Paradiso in Amsterdam, 1991.*

1993

In the meantime, other problems began to loom over the album's release, especially in relation to the cover, another "birth" from the Cobain-brain: the image of a transparent anatomical mannequin with faithful female features, but with wings on her back. Cobain also created the collage that constituted the back cover, described by him as "Sex and woman and In Utero and vaginas and birth and death." The piece portrayed small models of human fetuses and other model body parts spread out in a bed of orchids and lilies. The collage was created on the floor of the living room at Cobain's house and it was photographed by Charles Peterson, whom Cobain had unexpectedly called and asked to come over. The titles of the tracks on the album and the illustrations from *The Woman's Dictionary of Symbols and Sacred Objects*, a book written by feminist Barbara G. Walker, were added later to frame the image. It wasn't an eye-catching cover, indeed many "thinking" people found it disturbing or even offensive. To the point that Walmart, whose distributive and commercial power was enormous in the U.S., decided not to put the "indecent" cover of *In Utero* on its virtuous shelves. Geffen wasn't too worried. In the past, other albums had sold well, even without placement on those stiff aisles, and Nirvana manager Danny Goldberg was ready to support the band's freedom of expression. Surprisingly, Cobain was the one to suddenly fold: as a boy, Walmart was the only place where he could buy music, so he wanted kids in 1993 to be able to do the same with his music. The umpteenth proof of the sympathetic relationship (even if also problematic) that the artist had with his fans, even the mainstream audience that Nirvana had just won over and towards which he had an extremely conflicted outlook. So, a new back cover without fetuses was printed for Walmart and Kmart. But it didn't end there: the "Rape Me" track title ruffled the feathers of large-scale distribution "censors." So, having discarded Cobain's ironic suggestion to rename the fourth track on the album "Sexually Assault Me," it became, at least at Walmart, "Waif Me," a meaningless neologism but phonetically similar to the incriminated command, while remaining impossible to accuse of "instigating rape." The censored "variant" versions would be available two months after the official album came out, however.

Anyone who had imagined a drop in tension or creativity was proved wrong by an album that, in Cobain's vision, was meant to be the "best" by Nirvana, in terms of writing, execution and production. For many fans, *In Utero* was also better than *Nevermind*. The track listing is impressive: "Serve the Servants" with its autobiographical references and "Scentless Apprentice," a reference to Grenouille, the Luciferian protagonist of the novel *Perfume* by Patrick Süskind, about a great seventeenth-century French perfumer without his own body odor, who also was a serial killer.

There there's "Rape Me," one of the most powerful vocal performances by Cobain; "Frances Farmer Will Have Her Revenge on Seattle," a reference to the unlucky Hollywood actress Frances Farmer (Cobain also named his daughter after her), who suffered inhuman psychiatric treatment in the 1940s because of her rebellious behavior; the extraordinary "All Apologies" ("What else should I be? / All apologies / What else could I say? / Everyone is gay / What else could I write? / I don't have the right"), the second single and the song in which Cobain gives the world all his apologies for not being anything but himself, with ineliminable flaws and paranoias, incapable of simple happiness, unable to settle for a boring life or not to find challenges and complexity in every single thing. It's followed by "Pennyroyal Tea," "Dumb," "Very Ape" and "Tourette's," where the lyrics capture the confusion of not knowing which road to take and having to choose a direction, while also having the sensation that everything is out of your control. The frustration of having a bad heart, a "cold heart," and of not being able to overcome that feeling. Up to the conclusive "Milk It": "I am my own parasite / I don't need a host to live," an exploration of self-reflection and personal struggles. Beautiful songs, edgy rock, and visionary, incredible lyrics. Most of the songs offered clear insight into his existential malaise, into his dual relationship of attraction/repulsion to the world of pop stardom, into the celebration/denigration of the punk orthodoxy that gave rise to Nirvana and its clichés, the struggle to relate to the rest of the world, to "normal" people, who seemed, at least to those who belonged to that close and painful inner circle of sensitive and dissociated geniuses (Jim Morrison, Janis Joplin, Jimi Hendrix, Tim Buckley, Nick Drake, Ian Curtis, Amy Winehouse, Dolores O' Riordan and now also Sinead O' Connor) to be a species of monstruous, threatening alien-cockroaches, as Cobain's friend Burroughs would have described them.

In any case, regardless of all the hardships listed here, and of the repeated (though denied) relapse of the frontman into the spirals of heavy drug use, *In Utero* officially hit stores on September 21, 1993, less than a year after *Incesticide*. It sold 180,000 copies in the first week alone, immediately topping the Billboard charts (even without the sales from Walmart and Kmart), going gold in eight countries and platinum in nine, including the main markets of the U.S. and Great Britain. It didn't reach the sales heights of *Nevermind*, but it still sold five million copies in the U.S., plus an equal number around the world, despite being a harder and less compromising album than its precursor—and lacking a single as irresistible as "Smells Like Teen Spirit."

It should be said that, by then, Cobain truly had it all: fame, success, money, love, a family, limitless creativity, a future full of opportunity ahead of him. Yet, as *Seattle Weekly* wrote, Cobain remained "a tormented soul, a maelstrom of self-pity, intolerant pride, morbid introspection, ingenious self-delusion, merciless self-knowledge, showbiz revulsion, starstruck effusion, Faustian ambition, otherworldly detachment, and an iron will helpless to help itself." Incredibly, despite wanting to be successful, it was precisely being successful that caused so much inner conflict in Cobain. As he wrote in his journal: "Oh Pleez GAWD, I cant handle the success. Oh the success! The guilt! The guilt! Oh, I feel so incredibly guilty! Guilty for abandoning our true comrades, the ones who are devoted, the ones who have been into us since the beginning, the ones who, in ten years … will still come to see NIRVANA at reunion gigs at amusement parks, sponsored by depends diapers, bald fat and still trying to rawk. Saturdays: puppet show, rollercoaster & Nirvana…I hope I die before I turn into Pete Townshend."

The answer to all this malaise was always drugs, one in particular: heroin. Cobain was unable to liberate himself from its grip, and the drug was stopping him from having a "normal" life, the kind he said he wanted to have. Both he and Love tried to break free of it and, at a certain point, it seemed like they had managed. At least that's what newspapers at the time were saying. In Italy, *La Repubblica* wrote: "Recently, the couple that has most frequently ended up in the headlines for having drug problems are the 'terrible spouses' of American rock, that is, Kurt Cobain, leader of Nirvana (currently number one on the charts in the United States and in England with their new album, *In Utero*), and Courtney Love, who is also a rock musician with her band Hole, proud parents of a beautiful little girl.

A happy moment for the Cobain family at the MTV Video Music Awards, held at the Universal Amphitheatre, Universal City, California, on September 2, 1993.

Both have felt the depths of drug addiction, getting out in different ways: Courtney just before getting pregnant and Kurt almost exactly coinciding with the birth of their daughter. 'I didn't choose to have a child to get off heroin,' Courtney Love said to English monthly *Vox*. 'But I knew that I was at a turning point, that if I kept going, I would end up like those junkies you see on the streets, with tracks even on their neck, urban debris that no one cares for. If I've ever seen Satan, it looks like heroin, it's that insidious, tempting, it doesn't look like the devil with horns, but it has the air of an angel that promises you another paradise.'" After getting clean, Cobain wanted to tell his experience to a journalist, Michael Azerrad, to make a book, *Come as You Are*, "to do something helpful for others," Cobain stated. "To make sure someone else didn't find themselves in the same situation I found myself in, shooting up $100 of heroin in one go and not even feeling the effects. The next step would have been to start doing speedballs, a mix of cocaine and heroin which had killed John Belushi, but I realized I had a life to live, good or bad as it may be, and that it didn't make any sense to keep filling up needles to kill myself with. I had begun to be able to survive, not to die."

Kurt Cobain while recording MTV Unplugged in New York, *November 18, 1993.*

Cobain truly seemed "reborn." He said that the birth of his daughter was the greatest thing that had ever happened to him, that just holding her in his arms lit up his world. After having spent some time in rehab, he often said that he truly had been given new life. On July 22, he responded to Jon Savage, who had asked if he was feeling better: "Yeah. Especially in the last year, since I've been married and had a child, my mental and physical states have improved almost 100 percent. I'm really excited about touring again. I haven't felt this optimistic since right before my parents' divorce." Yet, little more than a month before, on June 4, the police had been called by the neighbors to stop a fight between Kurt and Courtney that had become particularly violent. Apparently, the fight started because Cobain was keeping guns in the house and Love wasn't having it. Their disagreement grew in volume and violence, until, say those who "in the know," Kurt went so far as to put his hands around Courtney's neck. Cobain was arrested and the guns confiscated, though he stayed in prison just three hours: "Not true at all," Love said to the press. "That's what our life is like now. If we so much as drink a beer, we end up in the newspapers." Love maintained that it was a misunderstanding with the neighbors: "We were playing punk rock in the garage and someone called the cops." Though she did confirm that officers of the law did confiscate a Colt AR-15 and a semi-automatic weapon, guns that she certainly didn't want to see in the house. Cobain also denied everything. Again, to Savage, he explained his side of things: "Total bullshit. That's another thing that has made me want to just give up. I never choked my wife, but every report, even *Rolling Stone*, said that I did. Courtney was wearing a choker. I ripped it off her, and it turned out in the police report that I choked her. We weren't even fighting. We weren't even arguing, we were playing music too loud, and the neighbors complained and called the police to us. It was the first time they'd ever complained, and we've been practicing in the house for a long time...See, there's a new law, which was passed that month in Seattle, that says that when there's a domestic violence call, they have to take one party or the other to jail. So the only argument Courtney and I got into was who was going to go to jail for a few hours. And they asked us, out of the blue, 'Are there any guns in the house?'...I have an M-16 and two handguns. They're put away, there are no bullets in them, they're put in the closet, and they took them away. I can get them back now. I haven't bothered to get them back yet, but it was all just a ridiculous little situation. It was nothing. And it's been blown up out of proportion. It's just like I feel like people don't believe me. Like I'm a pathological liar. I'm constantly defending myself...Sure. Courtney and I fight. We argue a lot. But I've never choked my wife. It's an awful f**king thing to be printed, to be thought of you...You know, we haven't had any problems, any bad re posts, any negative articles written about us in a long time. We thought we were finally over it—that our curse had worn itself out."

Kurt Cobain on stage in Modena, Italy, on February 21, 1993.

Meanwhile, on the *In Utero* tour, Nirvana had recruited a second guitarist, going back to a four-piece lineup for the first time since the Jason Everman days. That fourth element was, as we already mentioned, Pat Smear, the guitarist from the Germs, a band that ended even more lightning-fast than Nirvana, after the heroin overdose of singer Darby Crash. On some dates, there was even the cellist Lori Goldston and, for the concert at the Roseland Ballroom (on 52th Street in Manhattan), they successfully tried out a first acoustic set that lasted about 20 or so minutes.

Why mention this detail? Because it was the appetizer to a much richer dish: *MTV Unplugged in New York*. And why are those recordings, released by Geffen after Cobain's death, worth more to us than the other four official live albums, four compilations and three box sets released as part of the posthumous discography of the band? First of all, because, recorded just two months after the release of *In Utero* (November 18, 1993, at Sony Studios in New York), that live concert is the last tangible record of the entire band in great form. Moreover, because it offered a unique, stripped-down version of their usual noisy cocoon of rattling guitars and thundering drums, it was proof that Cobain had written a handful of "real" songs, the kind that could hold up even without the contribution of the original arrangements, the noise and everything else. That rare and impalpable substance that the songs of the Beatles, the Rolling Stones, Dylan, Pink Floyd, Lou Reed, and David Bowie are made of. The latter, of course, being someone that Nirvana's acoustic set paid tribute to with a vibrating cover of "The Man Who Sold the World," breathing new success into a single (taken from the 1970 album of the same name) that, until that moment, had never shone as brightly as it deserved to in the discography of the Thin White Duke. And indeed, it came out only in 1973 as a B-side to "Life on Mars." "We must have died alone / A long, long time ago," sang Kurt, probably feeling an elective affinity with the mysterious "man who sold the world." The song "represents how you feel when you're young, when you know that there's a part of you that you still haven't really put together yet," Bowie later explained. "You have this great searching, this great need to find out who you really are...It's a very sad rendition, of course because it is so tied up with his own life and death...I also remember, fairly clear, my state of mind when I was actually writing it, which was, I guess, as near to a mystical state that a 19-year-old can get into."

MTV Unplugged in New York was recorded on November 18, 1993, at Sony Studios in New York. It was a masterpiece.

The cover of MTV Unplugged in New York by Nirvana.

The two blonds, one English and one American, never met each other during Cobain's short career. But Bowie did comment on his version of the song: "I was simply blown away when I found that Kurt Cobain liked my work, and have always wanted to talk to him about his reasons for covering 'The Man Who Sold the World'" and tell him that "it was a good straightforward rendition and sounded somehow very honest...It would have been nice to have worked with him, but just talking with him would have been real cool." Of course, Nirvana's version had the knock-on effect of the track being added back to Bowie's set lists during his concerts in the 1990s.

Bowie aside, the *MTV Unplugged* concert contained five other cover songs. The first was "Jesus Doesn't Want Me for a Sunbeam" ("Jesus, don't want me for a sunbeam / Sunbeams are never made like me"), a new ode to Cobain's much-loved

Vaselines, who surely will never have earned as much as they did from the royalties coming from Nirvana's versions of their songs. "Plateau," "Oh Me" and "Lake of Fire" are all by the Meat Puppets (with Cris and Curt Kirkwood on stage with Nirvana), a tribute to the hardcore punk of their roots, also offered to the global MTV audience stripped to the bone of their usual sound. The last was a traditional folk song known primarily through the version by the great blues musician Leadbelly: "Where Did You Sleep Last Night?" which Kurt had already practiced with his friend Mark Lanegan years before. It was the closing track, in which, at the verse "I would shiver, the whole night through," his voice breaks and the band stops a second before the finale. "Unearthly, like a werewolf, unbelievable," Neil Young said of the performance. It was the performance that perhaps inspired him to dedicate his album *Sleeps with Angels* to Kurt.

The definitive track listing of the CD that is available today is 14 songs, of which eight are by Cobain (unconcerned about the exclusion of many Nirvana hits, first and foremost "Smells Like Teen Spirit"), plus six covers.

That live show, even with little time available for rehearsal, demonstrated that an acoustic turn was perceived by the singer as a possible evolution, an amplification of the sound of Nirvana. Cobain had even wanted to re-record it in the studio to release it outside of the MTV imprint, and he even floated the idea of a potential solo album to his manager, Danny Goldberg, received with the indulgence that every manager offers his stars to put them in the most favorable conditions to express their artistic vein (as he openly states in his book). Indeed, Goldberg comforted Cobain with a serene "why not?" giving him the example of none other than Neil Young. After all, for decades Young had been alternating albums in his own name with those recorded with Crazy Horse, then with Crosby, Stills & Nash (one, *Mirrorball*, even features grunge icons Pearl Jam!) etc., without it minimally damaging his relationship with the public and the overall perception of his astonishing songwriting. Goldberg has said that, with the *MTV Unplugged* show, Cobain was "dismantling the character that had made him

famous to keep his inner artist alive." Ju the "killer" of Ziggy Stardust, or Lennon Beatles. Unfortunately, that new path w unrealized possibility. In any case, with copies sold in the first week, immediate on the Billboard charts, and almost 13 m sold as of writing (eight million in the U. *Unplugged in New York* exceeded the sal and went gold in five countries, platinur seventeen.

COBAIN EVEN FLOA IDEA OF RELEASING ALBUM TO HIS MAN

Opposite: Kurt Cobain while filming MTV Unplugc
*Following pages: The band on stage at Sony Stud
18, 1993.*

COBAIN PUT A LOT OF
CARE AND DEDICATION
INTO THE RECORDING
OF THE *UNPLUGGED*
CONCERT

Also in the air was a potential collaboration with another one of his indie rock idols who had become a superstar, that is, Michael Stipe of R.E.M. In an interview, Cobain said he knew "what the next Nirvana album was going to sound like. Pretty, acoustic and with lots of strings." But what the future would have brought remains another "road to nowhere" open to the authors of speculative fiction.

The *In Utero* tour in the U.S. was a success in terms of ticket sales, but also an incredible theater of perdition. Many evenings, Cobain would get on stage in pretty bad shape, if not downright terrible. On others, the band was incredible and perfect. Many, too many, went to their concerts just to see what Cobain was capable of doing, what crazy antics he would pull on stage. Sometimes Cobain satisfied them, getting derailed, other times he was still in front of the microphone, singing without any apparent emotion. The last concert of the U.S. leg of the tour was in Seattle, at the end of which Cobain said multiple times that he didn't want to continue the tour in Europe. But by then, the show biz machine was already set in motion and running at full speed. Pearl Jam was at the height of its success with *Vs.*; Nirvana had to claim their rightful place, and the record label wanted *In Utero* to be a global hit. Cobain didn't want to play in Europe, but the tour began anyway in February. That was the beginning of the end. Cobain was tired, "every night his voice got worse," remembered Pat Smear. His relationship with Courtney Love was at an intense breaking point: their fights, even if only over the telephone, were devastating, and drug addiction did the rest. Every day was worse:

"I hated everything, all I did was hate everyone and everything," explained Courtney Love. "He couldn't take it anymore, he called me from Spain crying, he had reached his limit." Nirvana's last concert was on March 1 in Munich in an old airplane hangar called Terminal 1. The place wasn't much to look at, the acoustics were terrible, Cobain didn't take part in the sound check, probably to go look for drugs. Before the concert, he had a very tense phone call

The last Nirvana concert was held on March 1, 1994, in Munich. Then the tour was canceled

with his wife. Once the concert was over, having forced his voice in every single way, the tour was interrupted, completely canceled, wiping out all subsequent dates: Cobain was taken to a doctor, who diagnosed severe laryngitis and severe bronchitis, telling him that he wouldn't be able to sing for another two months so that his throat could heal. In the meantime, Cobain had lost weight, his relationship with Novoselic and Grohl was reduced to a bare minimum, and the only person in the band that he had a consistent relationship with was Pat Smear. And indeed, it was with him that, after another pacifying phone call with his wife, Cobain came to Rome, met there by Courtney Love and little Frances Bean.

Previous pages: A portrait of Cobain while recording MTV Unplugged *in New York.*

Opposite: Cobain playing at Markthalle, Hamburg, November 11, 1991.

On the night between March 3 and 4, 1994, the singer and his wife were in their room at the Excelsior Hotel, where they ordered room service complete with champagne. Their daughter was with them too. The next morning, when Courtney woke around 5:30, she found Kurt on the floor near the bed, unconscious and with blood dripping from his nose. According to the headlines, in addition to food and alcohol, that night Cobain had also ingested a massive dose of Rohypnol, a drug with hypnotic, anxiolytic and sedative effects, used to treat insomnia, but that also could be addictive and could become a true "drug" with devastating results, especially if taken together with alcohol and other narcotics. According to Courtney Love, that night Cobain took about 50 pills, causing him to overdose. She immediately called the hotel reception desk, which in turn called an ambulance. Cobain was swiftly taken to the Umberto I hospital, where he had his stomach pumped. After that, he was transferred to the American Hospital, where he woke up a few hours later. It was a foreboding event, symbolic of the tragic turn that the grunge idol's life had taken, about which there has been much speculation as to whether it was an accident or a first suicide attempt. "It was an excessive dose of painkillers and alcohol that put Cobain in a coma," said his American manager, Janet Billig, in the afternoon, while Cobain was in intensive care at the Rome American Hospital. The couple tried to shield Cobain from the assault of journalists coming from just about everywhere, having rushed there to see what truly was happening for themselves. In the morning, he seemed to be in "very grave condition,"

ON THE NIGHT BETWEEN MARCH 3 AND 4, 1994, KURT COBAIN FELL ILL IN ROME AND WAS TREATED AT THE ROME AMERICAN HOSPITAL. HE WAS IN A COMA AND COULD HAVE DIED

according to the first update from the doctor. Then the rumors started to swirl: better in the early afternoon, then a new low, and a sequence of essentially unconfirmed reports. Geffen, the singer's record label, released a statement on the matter: "He's in a coma. He collapsed due to exhaustion and the flu, further complicated by the singer having mixed alcohol and psychotropic drugs."

The specter of a legendary death even for the last rock hero vanished at four in the afternoon, when the news that his fans who had gathered in front of the hospital hoped for arrived: "Kurt has opened his eyes and is doing better. Even if he can't speak lucidly, he can move his hands. His wife and daughter, Frances Bean, are with him," said Billig, noting that Cobain took medicine to deal with the pain of his ulcer. No street drugs it seems for the singer who had admitted with transgressive honesty that he took heroin to treat his stomach pain. No, his managers spoke only of an excessive dose of painkillers. True? False? Does it make a difference? Out of nowhere, Cobain had decided to take three days off to enjoy a bit of peace, leaving a whirlwind tour that was destroying him and that he didn't want to continue. In Rome, he visited the Colosseum, the Vatican, and he's even smiling in the pictures, like a random tourist.

After all, he was on holiday in Rome, staying at the Excelsior, arriving two days earlier from Munich and ready to depart for Prague. The newspapers and television shows were reporting what had happened. "His wife was the one who saved him," stated the doctors, not so much for having called an ambulance right away, but for the instructions she provided to the EMTs about what and how much of it he had taken. "His wife saw him lose consciousness and immediately called for help. Her immediate action prevented the side effects of the loss of consciousness from taking hold. In these conditions, it's possible for gastric contents to end up in the lungs, and then…" explained Dr. Galletta, the head of the intensive care unit where Cobain was being treated. "In any case, he didn't go into a coma because of heroin. The alcohol amplified the effects of pharmaceuticals that, moreover, had been prescribed by his doctors." In the end, Cobain recovered, and he and Love went home. A few months later, in an interview with David Fricke of *Rolling Stone*, Love said that she believed it was his first suicide attempt: "He took 50 f**king pills. He probably forgot how many he took. But there was a definite suicidal urge, to be gobbling and gobbling and gobbling." The desire to die already was there, and unfortunately today we can say it with certainty: music was no longer enough to compensate for the desperation, the pain and the anxiety that had once again dominated his life. Despite just a few months before having said, "Frances Bean has completely changed my whole outlook on everything…I wasn't nearly as self-destructive as has been reported. I was doing drugs for a while…It's a part of my life that I'm not too proud of. It's been going on for years. I wanted to be a junkie for a few months after *Nevermind* and the tour. It was a really stupid idea. I didn't understand how evil it is, how hard it is to get off it." But Kurt also said he didn't want to die: "I'm not in any way afraid of death. I'm afraid of dying now. I don't want to leave behind my wife and child…I don't want to die. I've been suicidal most of my life. I didn't really care if I lived or died, and there were plenty of times when I wanted to die, but I never had the nerve to actually try it."

1993

Above, opposite and following pages: A few moments from the MTV Live and Loud performance, a concert held at Pier 48 in Seattle on December 13, 1993.

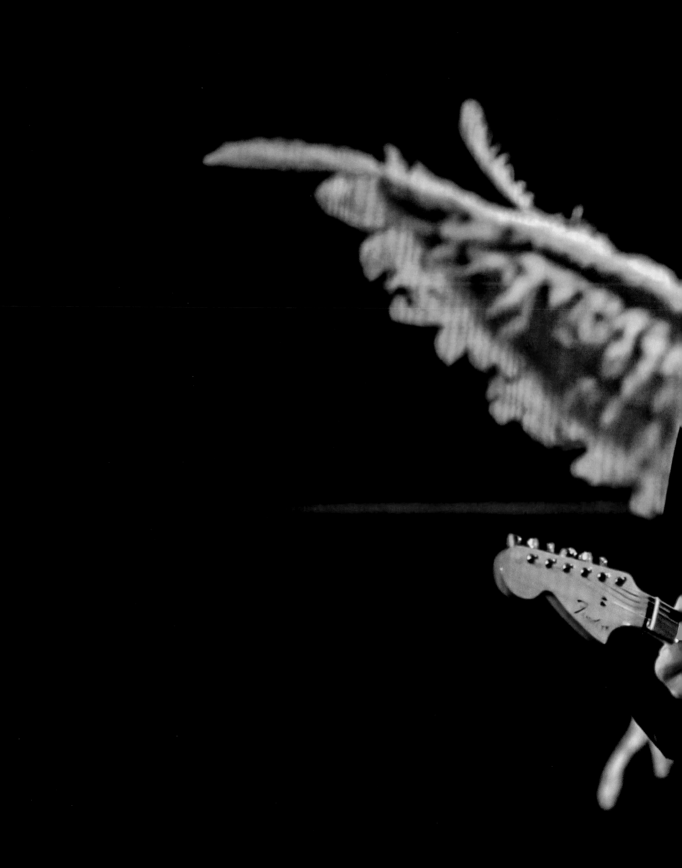

Opposite and above: Kurt Cobain playing with Nirvana on November 14, 1993, at the Coliseum in New York.

Kurt Cobain on stage at the Palatrussardi arena
in Milan, February 25, 1994.

Above and opposite: The concert on New Year's Eve, December 31, 1993, at the Oakland-Alameda County Coliseum Arena in Oakland, California.

Above and opposite: Two photographs of Krist Novoselic, Kurt Cobain and Dave Grohl goofing around in 1993.

LAUGH HARD
AT THE ABSURDLY EVIL

SAYOR KINDNES
BECAUSE CRUE
S ALWAYS POS
LATER

Kurt Cobain on a street in New York, 1993.

1993

Above: Kurt Cobain lighting a cigarette with Dave Grohl, 1993.

Opposite: A playful portrait of the Nirvana singer and frontman from that same year.

1994

Actually, in those days in Rome it was clear that no matter how much love, no matter how much happiness he might have in life, Kurt Cobain was always teetering on the edge, always in danger, with one finger on the self-destruct button, like in a space ship in a science-fiction movie, a rocket launched into the rock heavens, a mixture of dreams, visions, misery and galactic despair.

Once back in the U.S., Cobain agreed to enter a rehab program at the Exodus Medical Center in Los Angeles, but he didn't last long, just one day. Kurt went outside to smoke a cigarette, climbed over the wall of the property, went to the airport and hopped on a flight to Seattle. Once there, Cobain hid his tracks well. His wife couldn't find him, so she went as far as hiring a private investigator, to no avail.

Cobain was always at risk, always on the brink, his finger at the ready on the self-destruct button

On April 7, the band canceled their act at Lollapalooza, without having talked to Cobain, who had effectively disappeared. On April 8, an electrician hired to install security cameras in Cobain's house on Washington Boulevard in Seattle found him, dead. Kurt Cobain had killed himself at 27 years old. The coroner established a precise date: April 5, 1994. The singer who had sold 75 million albums had committed suicide at the age of 27 on April 5, 1994, with a shotgun. Next to his body was a long suicide note, written "To Boddah" (not Buddha spelled incorrectly, as Love initially thought, but his childhood imaginary friend, as his mother, Wendy, pointed out). In it, Kurt recounted his deep discomfort as the hypersensitive individual he was and, incredibly, the lack of enthusiasm in continuing his own very successful work as a musician, which is well summarized in the Neil Young song he quoted in the letter: "it's better to burn out, than to fade away."

"

To Boddah

   Speaking from the tongue of an experienced simpleton who obviously would rather be an emasculated, infantile complainee. This note should be pretty easy to understand. All the warnings from the Punk Rock 101 Courses over the years, it's my first introduction to the, shall we say ethics involved with independence and the embracement of your community has been proven to be very true. I haven't felt the excitement of listening to, as well as creating music, along with really writing something for too many years now. I feel guilty beyond words about these things, for example when we're backstage and the lights go out and the manic roar of the crowd begins. It doesn't affect me in the way which it did for Freddie Mercury, who seemed to love and relish the love and admiration from the crowd, which is something I totally admire and envy. The fact is, I can't fool you, any of you. It simply isn't fair to you, or to me. The worst crime can think of would be to pull people off by faking it, pretending as if I'm having one 100% fun.

   Sometimes I feel as though I should have a punch-in time clock before I walk out on-stage. I've tried everything within my power to appreciate it, and I do, God believe me, I do, but it's not enough. I appreciate the fact that I, and we, have affected, and entertained a lot of people. I must be one of the narcissists who only appreciate things when they're alone. I'm too sensitive, I need to be slightly numb in order to regain the enthusiasm. But, what's sad is our child. On our last three tours, I've had a much better appreciation of all the people I've known personally, and as fans of our music.

   But I still can't get out the frustration, the guilt, and the sympathy I have for everybody.

There is good in all of us, and I simply love people too much. So much that it makes me feel too sad. The sad little sensitive unappreciative Pisces Jesus man! why don't you just enjoy it? I dont know! I have a goddess of a wife who sweats ambition and empathy, and a daughter who reminds me to much of what I use to be. full of love and joy, every person she meets because everyone is good and will do her no harm.

And that terrifies me to the point to where I can barely function. I can't stand the thought of Frances becoming the miserable self destructive, deathrocker she become. I have it good, very good, and I'm grateful, but since the age of seven, I've become hateful towards all humans in general. Only because it seems so easy for people to get along and have empathy. Empathy only because I love and feel for people too much I guess. Thank you from the pit of my burning nauseas stomach for your letters and concern during the last years. I'm too much of a neurotic moody person and I don't have the passion anymore, so remember, it's better to burn out, than to fade away.

Peace, love, empathy,

Kurt Cobain

Frances and Courtney, I'll be at your altar.

Please keep going Courtney.

For her life which will be so much happier without me.
I LOVE YOU. I LOVE YOU! //

THE AUTHOR

ERNESTO ASSANTE began working in journalism in 1977. In his forty-plus-year career, he collaborated with numerous weekly and monthly Italian and international publications, including *Epoca*, *L'Espresso* and *Rolling Stone*. He conceived of and oversaw the "Music," "Computer Valley" and "Computer, Internet and More" supplements for *la Repubblica*. He was the author of books on music criticism, a few of which were co-written with his colleague Gino Castaldo. In 2005, the two created "Lezioni di Rock: Viaggio al Centro della Musica" (Lessons in Rock: A Voyage into the Heart of Music). From 2003 to 2009, he taught New Media Theory and Technique, followed by Analysis of Musical Styles, at La Sapienza University in Rome as part of the Communication Sciences curriculum. He taught the History of Popular Music at the Milan Conservatory. For White Star, he wrote multiple books on music that have been published all around the world.

The author would like to thank Mario Gazzola in particular, whose research was essential to the creation of this book.

Photo Credits

Project editor

Valeria Manferto De Fabianis

Graphic design

Paola Piacco

WS whitestar™ is a trademark property of White Star s.r.l.

© 2024 White Star s.r.l.
Piazzale Luigi Cadorna, 6
20123 Milan, Italy
www.whitestar.it

Translator: Katherine Kirby
Editor: Abby Young

ISBN 978-88-544-2081-6
1 2 3 4 5 6   28 27 26 25 24

Printed in China